A Commentary on
ECCLESIASTES

A Commentary on

ECCLESIASTES

David Pawson

Anchor Recordings

First published in Great Britain in 2019 by
Anchor Recordings Ltd
Synegis House, 21 Crockhamwell Road,
Woodley, Reading RG5 3LE

**For more of David Pawson's teaching,
including DVDs and CDs, go to
www.davidpawson.com**

**FOR FREE DOWNLOADS
www.davidpawson.org**

**For further information, email
info@davidpawsonministry.org**

ISBN 978-1-911173-98-4

Printed by Ingram Spark

Contents

This book is based on a series of talks. Originating as it does from the spoken word, its style will be found by many readers to be somewhat different from my usual written style. It is hoped that this will not detract from the substance of the biblical teaching found here.

As always, I ask the reader to compare everything I say or write with what is written in the Bible and, if at any point a conflict is found, always to rely upon the clear teaching of scripture.

David Pawson

Read Ecclesiastes 1:1–11

When you read through the book of Ecclesiastes, your first reaction is, "What on earth is that book doing in the Bible?" Have you had that reaction? It seems to put an emphasis on fate rather than faith, on happiness rather than holiness, on this world rather than the next, on things material rather than things spiritual. It is an odd sort of book. Some find it depressing rather than inspiring and go away really feeling down in the mouth after reading this writer. "Life is useless, utterly useless, all useless" – that is not quite where he ends, but it is where he begins.

There have been those who say, "You know, this isn't Bible teaching at all. This has more in common with either ancient Greek stoicism or oriental Buddhism or even modern existentialism but it is not the truth of God. This is not how God talks; it doesn't fit. It doesn't quote the prophets, for example, nor the rest of the Bible. It is nowhere quoted in the New Testament." So some people have said it should not be there at all. Funnily enough, when the Jews put the Old Testament together and when the Christians put the whole Bible together, neither group had any doubts that this book should be in. So if we have doubts, we have got to ask if there may be something wrong with us and if we may have missed the point of this book. To others it seems as if it is a statement of utter despair.

I read another book – not this one, and not part of the Bible – and I came across this sentence in it: "Nature has let us down. God has taken the receiver off the hook, and time is running out." That is a depressing statement if ever there was one. It seemed to me to be very much of a piece with Ecclesiastes. A comedian on television said: "Death is nature's way of telling you to slow down." That kind of sick humour is very close to some of the things this writer says. He says, for example: "Remember that no matter how long you live you will be dead much longer." What is this doing in the Word of God? Well I want to begin by saying this was written by a man who used his brain – a man prepared to think. It has been said that the greatest unexplored territory is right underneath your hat – meaning that most of us never stop to think. The majority of people in Britain are not stopping to ask the basic questions.

The basic questions always begin with "why", not "how". People ask :"How can I be happy? How can I make a living? How can I get guidance? How can I do this?" They should be asking, "Why should I make a living? Why should I need guidance?" Science answers the question "how" again and again, but it never answers the question "Why?" It may be able to tell us how the world began, but it doesn't tell us why, and it is the "why" that is important. This is a book to tell you why, and that is much more important than how.

The writer of this book was someone who sat down and thought about life. He was an older man, and he was looking back over a lifetime spent searching for the answers and a lifetime in which he had failed to find them. He says, "I set out in life to find out what life is all about." Here is the big question which is being asked in this whole book: is life worth living? A crude and silly answer to that is, "It depends on the liver" (from someone who meant it in more senses than one). Your health is everything, but it isn't. Even if you have your health and your liver is in order, why live?

I remember somebody being asked, "Why are you working at that?"

"Well, I'm working at this to get money."

"Why?"

"Well, you've got to live."

"Why?"

The man had no answer, and there he was working every day to make a living, to live, and he had never asked why. Why bother to keep going? Why work just to go on working? Why get up and go to work and come home and get your tea and put your feet up and go to bed and get up and go to work and come home, get your tea, put your feet up, go to bed, get up the next morning, go to work.... Why is it worth it? What do you have to show for it at the end? That is the question, and he asks here, "What profit is there to a man who has worked hard all his life? What does he have to show for it at the end? What is there left at the end of life?" Because it is what is left at the end of the day that is profit.

Not only did this man ask the question, but Jesus asked it: what shall it profit a man when he gets to the end of the day and adds up the books? Will it be profit or loss? That is the question. Is life worth living? This book is written by an old man but it is addressed to people between the age of fifteen and twenty-five. Here is an old man pleading with young people all the way through: find the answer at the beginning of your life; don't wait until you get to my age; think through these dead ends before you go down them; find out where life is meant to lead before you discover that you have wasted your years going up a cul-de-sac – that is what his message means.

At the end of the book he makes an impassioned plea to young people. He says: before your hair is as grey as mine is, before you are doddery, before you are elderly, before you are senile, get the answers to these questions.

There are many people who only start asking the right questions after they have discovered all the dead ends. We are going to go on this search with this man, and one of the things I like about him is his absolute honesty. He tells us he tried this, he tried that, he tried the other – things that people are trying today.

We say to the older generation, "We've nothing to learn from you," and we go and learn the same lessons they had to learn the hard way. We find out that the things we thought promised life are literally dead ends. Praise God for somebody in the Bible who was honest enough to write it down in old age and say: you name it—I have tried it and I did not find the meaning of life. Life was not worth living even though I tried it. So this book of the Bible has got something to say.

To put it in a nutshell, Ecclesiastes asks all the right questions but it comes up with the wrong answers – that is why you disagree with some of its statements – and I want to ask why this is. The answer to that is fairly simple: he decided to look for the meaning of life within two very distinct limits, and once you put those limits on life, you condemn yourself to finding the wrong answers.

First of all, he put a limit in space on his search. He looked for the meaning of life under the sun. That is a key phrase occurring twenty-eight times in this short book of twelve chapters. He said, "I've tried everything under the sun," and that phrase is still used. He says, "I have looked everywhere under the sun," and this was why he came up with the wrong answers. Because once you say "under the sun" you have shut yourself off from the answer to your question as to the meaning of life.

You see, the phrase "under the sun" means "everything within our observable world, everything that we can see at ground level, everything in the sphere in which we live and move". Once you say, "I'm going to look for the meaning of life 'under the sun'" you condemn yourself to saying life is pointless, useless; it is not worth living. This man is being absolutely honest that those who live under the sun, whose highest ambition is to get a suntan, will find out that it is a dead end and that that way does not bring the meaning of life. Living under the sun, looking everywhere under the sun, doing anything under the sun, you will fail to find a purpose to life.

Now the second limitation that he imposed on his own search was this: it was a limitation in time. In other words, he was going to find it here somewhere in this observable universe. He also put a limit on time, and another key phrase that comes in again and again is "as long as I live". This man had no concept of life after death. Time and again he asks the question: "Who can tell me what will happen to me when I die?" Nobody, there is no answer to that. Therefore he says he has got to find the meaning of life in this life.

These two limits, "under the sun" and "while I live", prevented him from ever coming up with the right answers. This book is saying loud and clear, and God wanted it in the Bible, that if you are a secular man, if you are humanist, if you are bounded in time and space by what you can observe and by how long you live, you can only come at the end of the day to one conclusion: life is useless. If you are honest with yourself at the end of the day, you will say that it has been pointless, a waste of time.

Now that is an honest statement, and praise God that he begins where we are, and the Bible begins where you are, and what I am writing now may be precisely what you think, especially if you are an older person. You are beginning to be disappointed and disillusioned. You set out as this man did, with high hopes that life would fulfil its promise. Life was full of promise, you built your castles in the air, and you finished up with a bungalow in Bournemouth. You are disillusioned and you wonder how long you will be fit enough to dig the garden. Can you get the feel, the guts of the man as he honestly says: I set out like you; I was going to live life to the full. I tried pleasure; I tried money; I tried fame; I tried education; I tried everything – I have finished up a disillusioned, disappointed man who says I have nothing to show for it at the end of the day; I have no profit in the accounts of life; I have nothing left now that my little day is over.

There is honesty for you. You don't need to go outside the Bible to find humanism and secularism portrayed in utter, stark honesty.

Now there is this one difference. Though he does say utterly frankly, "I do not know the answers to the questions of life, I don't understand life. I cannot tell you why it is worth living," nevertheless he is not an agnostic. As a Jew he knew that there was a God. He doesn't argue for the existence of God. Like the Bible as a whole, he assumes there is a God. The word "God" comes in now and again. People say, "Well surely he is reaching above the sun there" – no, he isn't. He says that God is above the sun, and is sure that God must have the answers to these questions but is not answering, and has not told him the secret, so he can't tell us.

He believes that in the long run it must be better to fear God, but he can't tell us why; he believes it must pay to be good but he says that all the facts of life tell him that it doesn't. Throughout this book there is a tension in this man stemming from his understanding of the faith he was brought up to believe was true: that there is a God and that he is just and fair and that to God life does matter, and that there is a meaning to life. On the other hand there was this feeling: he has not told me; I have had to search for myself, and I have not found, and I just don't know. On that basis he was going to give young people some advice as to how to cope with a world that they don't understand – how to make something of a life the meaning of which eludes them.

If that was all I had to preach, I don't think I would bother to preach it. But we will look into this book and I am going to finish up by showing you how our Lord Jesus Christ both contrasts with and complements this man, and takes his questions and answers them, and takes his longings and fulfils them, and takes his dreams and makes them come true. You need to go through Ecclesiastes to find Christ. You need to go through some kind of experience in which you say: "I just see it all as pointless; I can't find meaning; I can't find life; I am not fulfilled; I am not satisfied." You need to go through that to hear Christ say: "This is life" to find out that it is all worthwhile after all, and that there is tremendous purpose and meaning to it.

Now I want to say a little about the writer; I am not going to go into all that the scholars say as to whether it is Solomon or not. His name certainly never occurs in the book, but he does describe himself as a son of David and the King of Israel living in Jerusalem. But he does give himself a very unusual title, *Qoheleth*, which originally meant an audience or a congregation or an assembly. Then it came to mean "the man who gathered them together". Then it came to mean "the speaker who was able to gather an audience". Then it came to mean "the lecturer" or "the professor" – thus, the *Philosopher*.

A philosopher is a person who likes the answers. "Philo" means "I love" and the "–sophy" part comes from *sophia*, wisdom – "I like to know". He wants answers from life. He wants to ask the questions and he wants an answer. I praise him for this. Far too many people go right through life without ever asking the right questions. That is why they never find Jesus Christ – they don't ask. Even if they expressed honest doubt they might get through to Jesus, but they don't.

Let me build up an identikit picture of this man's character,

15

if I can, from the book. First of all, I have pointed out that he is an old man. That is quite clear; he is a doddery old man, and he knows it. He speaks from almost a wheelchair. He is speaking to young people from the vantage point of someone who has seen it all and been around every corner. Secondly, he is an educated man. He is, in fact, upper class, if we can say that, from the background from which he speaks. He has had all the money he has needed to do anything. He has had all the education he could have asked for.

He is a very observant man; he watches life carefully. He is a detached observer, not prejudiced. He looks at a human situation, and he says: "This is the fact, however much it contradicts my faith, there is the fact." He is a godly man – he believes there is a God, and he doesn't argue the point, though he can't fit that faith into the facts. He is honest and hardworking and I get the impression of a dynamic, energetic character. Whatever he did, he did it to the hilt. He did things not in half measures; he went the whole hog. Whatever he tried, he went the whole way, so we see a real, exciting character, a respected man who younger people turn to for advice. I find a man who is willing to teach from his experience.

Looking at vv. 1–11 we see a pessimistic beginning. He states the conclusion that he has come to in answer to the big question "Is life worth living?" Then he begins to tell us why he has come to that conclusion. His conclusion is, "Life is useless." The older versions of the Bible had the word "vanity". But that word has begun to lose its meaning. It is a word meaning "emptiness", "hollow". The literal Hebrew word means "a wisp of breath". That is a very good description of life, isn't it? You begin to breathe and then you cease. Life is just a breath; it is gone.

It is almost the description of going out on a cold winter's morning and seeing your breath coming out of your mouth.

You see it come out, and then very quickly it disperses and disappears. Life is just a breath and it is gone. Or perhaps another translation would be "Life is just a bubble." A bubble is just a lump of air. You try and grasp it. It looks so beautiful; it has colour. You try and grasp it, and you are left with nothing.

Now, anybody who feels that life is just a bubble ought to read this book. Here was a man who grasped life and found it was just a bit of air – nothingness. I would have translated this as: "Life is pointless." That is the real flavour of what he is saying here: you have nothing to show for it at the end. You have nothing left at the end of the day.

The moment you die you draw a line under the accounts and you say, "Now, what have I got left that I can keep?" Because that is your profit. The answer is: "Nothing; I have worked so hard, and I have been so busy; it is so pointless." What a conclusion! Yet he is writing as an older man and he says: "Why have I come to that conclusion? I have come to that conclusion because everything I see is rushing in circles and getting nowhere." Life for him has been a treadmill or a roundabout. For some, life is like a roundabout. They get on; they have a great time while they're on. They go round and round and they get off just where they got on, and they have lost their money. For others, life isn't a roundabout but it is a treadmill. You get in and you go round and round. You tread your way to the office and back. But you get off just where you got on. Generations come and generations go, but the world stays just the same.

Is this not facing facts? Is this not being utterly honest? You will have nothing. "Ah," but someone will say – and people do say this to me: "I hope to leave the world a little better than I found it. I hope to leave something for those who come after me." Have you heard that? That is the hope that keeps many people going. They know that when they get to the end of the road, they will have nothing to take from this world. Naked they came into it; naked they go out. So they hope to leave something for the people who follow on.

"Ah," says this man, "face life honestly. Do you think you'll be remembered, and for how long? Do you think your little life will really make much difference to this world? Not a bit of it. You will have made no impression whatever on it. It will carry on without you. The seasons will come, and the seasons will go. People will be born, and people will die. The world will go on just the same as if you had never been on it." Hard talking, yes, but it is making people face facts. It is taking them to the logical conclusion of their own thinking. If you have hopes that you are going to leave this world a much happier, better place than you found it, then think again. It will have just as much war and famine, if not more, after you have gone than before you came.

"So if you think you're going to change the world," he says, "think again – that is not the meaning of life." He says that individual lives are like a piece of paper just thrown into the river, drifting down and then gradually disintegrating and sinking to the bottom. The river goes on flowing, just as it did before. Look not only at human life. People are born and die.

There was a ninety-year-old Christian doctor in Whitby, Yorkshire, and he was invited to speak to a youth club in which there were some very "with-it" youngsters. He gave them a talk for half an hour on his faith at ninety years of age and a young girl in a mini skirt got up and said, "Dr Vines, you're old-fashioned." He said, "My dear young lady, you came into the world in an old-fashioned way, and you'll go out of it an old-fashioned way." That is what is being said here. There is nothing new.

Look at nature, as distinct from human beings. The sun starts in the east, goes round to the west, then hurries round underneath to get up in the morning. Of course, the writer's astronomy may have been a bit astray but his observed facts were perfectly correct. He didn't know about evaporation in those days, but he said, "All the rivers go into the sea, and the sea is not full. It doesn't overflow, and somehow the water gets back to the beginning, and it flows all over again into the sea." It is like me getting up to go to work and going back to bed.

Or look at the wind. The weather forecaster says, "It's southwest today," and then it's northeast, and then it's southeast, and then it's northwest. It just goes round and round in circles – the same amount of air just going around in circles, getting nowhere. Indeed, the whole universe, we now know, is like this. We are all going in circles getting nowhere fast. You are moving at nineteen miles a second at this moment; can you feel it? You would if the Lord accelerated or slowed it down. We would all finish up stuck to a wall.

But you are getting nowhere fast; you are just going round in circles. That is why the sun rose this morning and will go to bed tonight, because we are just spinning round, getting nowhere fast. Believe you me, after your funeral it will be going round. You will have had no impression on it whatever. So life is pointless. Old Father Thames keeps rolling along. It has been rolling along since the Romans came. I read that when the people of London drink water they are drinking water that has already been drunk five times by five other people further up the Thames, and that river keeps rolling along just the same.

This philosopher looks at history. The eye can never see enough to be satisfied, and the ear can never hear enough. What does he mean? He is saying we are always searching for something new. What is the whole tourist package industry doing? Showing people new sights. Sightseeing – and the more sites we see, the less satisfied we are. There is another place we haven't been. So we spend our lives going to a different place on holiday, and we never see enough. There is always something newer, we think.

We never hear enough that's new, do we? We pay a fortune for our newspapers, and one Sunday paper is the same as the next. The wars shift from one country to another, divorces shift from one "celebrity" to another, but there is nothing new. The only reason we think news is new is because we don't remember when it happened previously. Is this not true? "History repeats itself" is a favourite proverb. So it was said in a book three thousand years ago: life is pointless. We are getting nowhere fast, going around in circles; history is going around in circles. You may know the French proverb "Plus ça change, plus c'est la même chose." What does it mean? The more things change, the more they turn out to be the same. That is a pretty negative way to begin. It is true. It is where you have to start if you are going to be honest about life.

Now, I find the people who argue about this conclusion are young, ambitious and quite sure they can make a mark on life. But it is not often that I find older people arguing with this conclusion. I am referring now to older people who have not found the answer to the question. They would say: "That describes how I feel." Men in their fifties have come to me and said, "Looking back on my working life, I cannot answer the question, 'What have I achieved?' When I retire and get my gold watch I won't be missed. Everything will carry on exactly as it was before." That is life for someone honest.

The Bible shows here that you can go down path after path to the very end and still come to a notice saying "no entry". The trouble is many people don't even think this far ahead. Jesus criticised such people. He taught that you are a fool if you only think in terms of what you can achieve in this life. You are a fool because this very night you will be told to add up the accounts, and you will have nothing to show for it – no profit. What shall it profit you if you have lived within this circumscribed framework under the sun? For as long as you live that way you are doomed to disappointment.

Will you learn from an old man? Are you willing to see Ecclesiastes as a warning sign? Are you willing to listen to an old man speaking the truth about all the very things that some young people are trying, hoping that they will bring real life? If you are willing to learn, then you could learn a much more positive thing. Some years ago I spoke to forty young people – all Christians. I asked them to write down on a piece of paper the one thing that had come into their life that they really valued more than anything else since they had met Jesus. Out of forty young people, interestingly thirty-eight wrote the same word independently. It was *purpose*.

Here is an old man saying "pointless", and here are thirty-eight young people saying "purpose". The old man knows what is a solemn truth: that the majority of people who find the answer to the question "Is life worth living?" find it in their youth.

That is why the old man writes to the young. That is why he teaches: Remember your Creator in the days of your youth before the years come when it is too late; find God now, and you will find life now. He is saying: I went all that way, and I couldn't get life related to God – the result was at the end of life my conclusion was that my life was pointless; I have been going in circles, getting nowhere fast.

I want to finish by quoting Jesus and Paul. Let me begin with Paul, a Jew from Tarsus. He was as honest with the facts as Ecclesiastes, and he agrees perfectly with what Ecclesiastes says. He wrote in Romans 8: "The whole universe has been subject to vanity, to futility." They are the same words – the whole universe has been subject to this. Why? Because human beings are not fit to live.

It means, therefore, that God has built this into our universe as it is now – that the whole thing is going in circles. Everything is futile. Everything is vanity. Everything is pointless. Everything is going round and round and getting nowhere fast. It is God who did that to our universe. It was not like that in the beginning. When God made the universe it was going somewhere. It was going in a line, not in circles, but it is God who has built in this futility to everything. Why? Because we are not yet fit to travel the road that leads to him. So the whole creation is subject to futility – waiting for what? Waiting for our redemption, waiting for something to get put right in us, waiting for us to be fit to live in the world and then God will make the world fit to live in, and will create a new heaven and a new earth. The new heaven and the new earth will not be going in circles, it will be travelling in a straight line. Do you get the big cosmic concept, the overview, here? Life is useless, pointless, circular, getting nowhere fast, and your little life on this planet is doing exactly the same thing. Don't kid yourself that you are going to leave this world better than you found it. It is going to go on just as it was, after you are gone.

You have got to find out a purpose for yourself, and you will find it by reaching above the sun. You will find it by reaching beyond this life, and only when you reach out in space and forward in time – beyond the limits that our scientific world has imposed on our thinking – will you do so. For our scientific and technological era teaches us to live within that frame. No wonder that in the technological era art, drama and music are all saying: "Life is meaningless." No wonder our culture is crying out in despair. No wonder we are getting sick humour. No wonder plays are coming out with no point – no story. They are saying: "There is no point; no meaning."

But the writer of this book did not take that position. He

said that there must be a meaning; he believed there is a God who knows that meaning. He just had not been able to get through to him and find it out. But the Christian is someone who can say: "I have got through and I have discovered the answer. God did have a meaning, and he did have a purpose, and now I know it." That's why a Christian could never write the book of Ecclesiastes, not unless he wrote it before he became a Christian and was a very honest person who was willing to face facts.

Look at some of the other things Paul said. "A Christian lives not below the sun; he lives in the heavenlies with Jesus, and life there is glorious." A Christian is actually living above the sun, not under it. He is basking in something much better than sunshine. It is a glorious life to live in the heavenlies, and if you are not a Christian you won't understand a word of what I have just stated.

But every Christian knows, according to Colossians, that our life is hid with Christ in God. Therefore, if you are risen with Christ, seek the things that are above, where he is, and you are – that is where life is. Furthermore, we are not living in a life that is bounded by birth and death. We are already living eternal life that stretches through the grave and cannot be touched by death.

So already there is a dimension that gives meaning and purpose, and every action of mine today and tomorrow is going to count and is going to leave its mark and will be remembered by God and by me. That has given a whole new dimension to life. I have got out of the circle, and I am now travelling along a line.

Jesus not only said "You fool" to a man who did not think beyond the parameters of this world; Jesus also said: "This is life, to know you [God], and to know Jesus whom you sent."

If you read the teaching of Jesus, he relates life here and now to the world above the sun and the world beyond the grave. Once you get those dimensions into your thinking, you have found the answer that this man never found. You say: "Life, pointless? It has only got a point now. I never saw the point of it before while I was rushing around that roundabout. Now I am off the roundabout and I am a pilgrim, and I am going somewhere. I know where I am going, and I know who goes with me."

Dr Pearson, a great preacher, once said: "The key to Ecclesiastes is that a man is too big for this world." Do you understand what he was saying? You cut life off at the level of the sun, and at the point of time, the grave, and you are too big to fit into that box. You stretch beyond it; you are cribbed, cabined, and confined within it, and you cannot spread your wings. You cannot live within that box. You may try, and you may kid yourself for years that you are having a great life. But I warn you that you will get to the point where you say of whatever the scene has been: "It is useless – promises, promises."

Then maybe you will remember a preacher once declared that if you looked above the sun and saw God, and if you looked beyond the grave and saw Jesus preparing another life for you, you would see that life here is a preparation, a pilgrimage. It is leading somewhere. It is not leading to six-feet under; it is leading to glory. Once you see that, Monday morning becomes a different day. Life is going somewhere. Do you know this is death to the philosophy of evolution? It is death to the optimistic humanist. That is why they hate the conclusion "life is useless" and they won't face it.

Those who believe that automatically the whole world is evolving and getting somewhere – rubbish. It is getting nowhere and God subjected it to that futility. We are not evolving anywhere. I think it would be a bold person who would say the world today is better than when Ecclesiastes was written. Are there fewer wars? Is there less suffering?

Can people get on with each other any better? It is just the same.

So the writer of Ecclesiastes picks us up by knocking us down. He is saying: follow your own thinking to its logical limit – until you have realised that life is pointless.

Then you will be ready to listen to another preacher called Jesus, who came to lift us above the sun and to give us life beyond the grave so that we could say: life is useful; there is a point – I can see it now.

Read Ecclesiastes 1:12–2:26

Here we have a philosopher, a thinker, who is king. He was the wealthiest and most intelligent king Israel ever had. He tells us about what he did. If you were King Solomon, and you had his brains, his money, power and status, what would you do with it?

Well, he tells you what he did with it. He says he would make a study of everything that people do in life to find out which pursuit makes life worth living. For remember that the question posed in Ecclesiastes is this: is life really worth living? Is there any point to it? Is there any meaning to my daily existence? Have I made any mark at all on planet earth having been here for sixty, seventy or eighty years? There are many things that we would love to try doing. There are places that we would like to visit. Would you like to try a parachute jump? We all have our little dreams and we have our own ideas locked up somewhere in our hearts. We feel somehow that doing something different might give us some clue to real living.

Solomon is saying: I am going to try them all to see if they really do give a clue to what constitutes real living. He was in the best possible position to try this because he was king. He was at the top and he started from the top. He was in a position to go all the way down each of the paths that he was told lead to life. He was going to try them one after the other and see if at the end of the road he could say: "I have really lived; I can tell you the secret of life."

Solomon was king of quite a large country, for Israel was

27

never so large a power as under King David, Solomon's father. Solomon had inherited that kingdom, at peace with its neighbours, and inherited the loyalty of an entire united nation. He inherited all the wealth which his father laid up for him. David had spent the last years of his life collecting silver, gold, timber and stone so that Solomon could really build the place up. When you have inherited all that and you have a chance to make use of it during your life – what an opportunity.

There are five points to make about this passage. One: there was his ambition to study everything that is done in the world, every path people try and to which they give their time, money and energy. He was going to try them all. He was in a position to do so. He did not have to fight wars. He did not have to work. He had plenty of money. He did not have to do it all himself – he had plenty of slaves. Having everything he wanted, he set off in what has been called "the search for satisfaction", which is a search that nearly everybody in the world is engaged in at this very moment.

The tragedy is that so very few people will learn from others in this search. We will all go down all these roads ourselves. There are millions today doing just what Solomon did and getting as far as he did – which was nowhere. For instead of keeping us in suspense until the end of his search, he tells us right before the beginning that he got absolutely nowhere.

The second thing that he shares with us is the answer to his question: Do these roads lead anywhere? In a vivid phrase he says that every one of them was like chasing the wind. Have you ever tried doing that? It is the most useless, pointless, senseless, purposeless occupation you could ever think of.

Can you imagine seeing a man chasing up the high street and you say, "What are you doing?" He replies, "I am chasing the wind. Since the wind is from the southwest today, I am chasing up the high street." When the wind is from the east, I chase down the high street. That is what you are doing if you are chasing any of the things that Solomon chased.

What fools we are to chase the wind – to grasp at something and find out that it is just a bubble, a lump of air. You will never catch the wind. "Got it!" You fool, you haven't caught the wind. It will just go on blowing without you. Even though you may have trapped a little bit of air in your hands, it is no longer the wind because it is not moving and you have not caught anything. That was his ambition and his answer is: what a miserable fate God has condemned us to. What a miserable life this is. You try everything and it finishes nowhere and he blames God for this frustration. He uses terms that bring a vivid picture to my mind. I am not sure they were in his mind because I don't know if jigsaws had been invented by then. But he says something like this: you can't make straight what is crooked; you can't count what isn't there. What he means is that this world is so crooked that nothing fits; this world is so hollow that nothing fills it. I got a picture in my mind as I read those two phrases, of a man with a box with no picture on the lid – a jigsaw inside and when he picked out the pieces he tried fitting them together and none of them would quite fit. He could not get the hang of any of them. On the box it said: "five-hundred pieces". So he counted them up and found four hundred. Can you imagine anything more frustrating or aggravating than that?

Everything is crooked and you can get nothing straight. Nothing goes in line, nothing fits. Everything is so hollow and there are pieces missing and you can't count what is not there. Life is like a jigsaw you cannot make up. This is being very honest and Solomon says: God, why did you give us life like this?

You may be critical of this man because he blames God, but I tell you he was blaming the right person. God did make life like a jigsaw puzzle in which some of the pieces don't fit and vital ones are missing. This man was right to say, "God, why?" For that is the question: why did God make life like this, because life is like this? I will give you the answer to that question at the end of this chapter because the New Testament gives an absolutely clear answer as to why God gave us a life that was like a jigsaw in which no pieces fit and in which many of the pieces are missing. You cannot straighten what is crooked and you cannot count what is not there. What a miserable fate. Here is a man who has had all the money, all the power, the top position, everything you could ask for, and has tried every way he can to live and that is his conclusion as a disillusioned old man. However he doesn't finish on a negative note. But now let us look at his search. My third point concerns his achievements. What did he try and how far did he get with them?

Well, the answer is that there are three main roads in life and just about everything people do can be put under one of these headings. There is the road of *enlightenment* – knowledge, education and learning. There is the road of *enjoyment*, in which you seek any pleasure you can, any thrill. There is, thirdly, the road of *enrichment*, in which you seek to enrich yourself and the world in which you live by acquiring things – by spending your money in certain ways. The last thing can be unselfish. For example, you could donate money to a university to help others by advancing medical research.

Everybody I meet is on one of the three roads. But Solomon was going to travel along all three. He tells us he went right down all of those roads until the bitter end. He said the end of each one of them was bitter. You need not give your life to a road that leads to a dead end.

The first one he mentions is the road of *enlightenment*. He says he set himself to study wisdom and knowledge. He had a great brain and he used that brain and he studied life. He was a man of observation; he was a man of insight. He was a man who could analyse a situation and could penetrate to the depths of it. He studied hard, he read books, and he read people, and he read life. He said that knowledge is the answer; wisdom is the answer. Then he said that gradually he began to be disillusioned with knowledge.

I heard a well-known professor in this country say, "We know more and more about less and less." He was expressing disillusionment. Indeed, the more educated you are, the more uneducated you feel you are. The more you know, the more you realise there is to know in whatever field it may be. We are now having to specialise more and more so that you have to narrow your field of interest if you are going to know anything today. Information, knowledge keeps increasing. The human memory is not big enough so we have to have computers to hold it all – knowledge, knowledge, knowledge. Where is it getting us? We know more and more about less and less.

Solomon, who was one of the cleverest people who ever lived, said, "I found myself lying awake at night having my mind kept awake because I knew too much. My mind was so teased with the questions I had not answered, I wanted to know more and more." Knowledge can be as much of an addiction as drugs. I could give you so many examples. Consider Henry Martin. When he received the highest honour that a scientist can receive, he said, "I have grasped a shadow." Humphrey Davey, a brilliant scientist who invented the safety lamp for miners and many another gadget, wrote in his later years, after his retirement: "I am very miserable." "The truth hurts," says Solomon. The more you know of it the more it hurts because the more you realise you don't know. To live for knowledge does not bring life. It is stimulating, it is interesting while you do it, but when

31

you get to the end of life, what can you do then with all your knowledge? Where does it go? It dies with you.

The second road he tried was the road of *enjoyment*. Having explored the avenue of the mind, he turned to the heart. From the intellectual, he turned to the emotional. From seeking enlightenment he sought enjoyment and he lived it up. He was in the middle of the wine-growing country and he could have any wine he wanted from the cellars of the palace. Women – he said: "I had as many as I wanted." He actually got through 1,300. He had sex with 1,300 women, with 300 of whom he went through a wedding ceremony. So if you think that is the answer – he tried it. He tried every pleasure he knew. He said: "Whatever I enjoyed, I took. I have tried it" – and he had. He went right down that road of enjoyment and he discovered the paradox of pleasure: the more you seek it, the less you have.

Yet somehow the whole search went stale on him. It wasn't all crude. There was refined song, there were orchestras, beautiful music. Somehow when he went down that road, whether it was crude or cultural, the road of living to enjoy himself went dead on him and he just did not get there. He didn't lose his head. He says, "I never lost my wisdom in all of this," and that is quite a claim. Many people lose their head when they just give full rein to their heart.

He says, "I gave wine to myself." He never says, "I gave myself to wine." Some people do that – they become its slave. He was exploring it and he pulled back. He had sufficient strength of will to pull back when he found it was a dead end, but he went right down it. He said that it did not satisfy him; he never had real joy, and even laughter became a kind of madness. He tried entertainment, he tried comedy, he tried everything. Then he saw how hollow it was to live for laughter and he became a kind of melancholic.

You can point to many comedians who found that. Tony

Hancock's suicide is a perfect example. Laughter is madness if that is all you have, and that is all that Tony Hancock did have, so the road was a dead end.

Let us turn to the third road that people try. This is the road of *enrichment*: in a very positive way, the joy of creativity, the joy of spending your money in a way that will make something last after you are gone. There is the joy of having an estate, of building a house. As the Chinese proverb goes: "If you want to be remembered, write a book, build a house, plant a tree or have a son." All these things will last after you have gone. Some of them require expenditure. Solomon set himself to create the kind of estate, the kind of metropolis that would be one of the wonders of the world, and he achieved it. He worked very hard, he supervised the planning, he sat with his architects and committee and he got it built. It was such a wonder that a queen travelled hundreds of miles, and that was quite something in those days. The Queen of Sheba had heard incredible tales of this man and of his metropolis, his garden, orchards, arboretum, his bulls and his palace. She came and said: "I wasn't told half."

He did it all, and he thought: "I'm enriching the world; I'm not just enriching myself. I'm enriching the country. I am putting things up that will make this country great." He got to the end of that and he said: "What has it achieved?"

What had it all done? The answer was that it didn't mean a thing. Now why did he say that? Why was he so disillusioned with this road of enrichment? There are three reasons and he now gives them. I will give you my fourth point for this passage: his aggravation. The Authorized Version has "vexation of spirit" – and that and "aggravated" really get it across. He was aggravated by it all. Why? There are three reasons that he gives for his aggravation. First, that he was simply doing what others had done before him. He had got not one inch further than other great kings. When you study history, that is what you find.

When you look at the ruins of the Roman Forum, that is an experience. From there you can see the Palace of Caligula, the Senate House, and the Arch of Titus. You see how each of them wanted to build and enrich. If you go to Athens, you look at the Parthenon, climb Mars Hill and you look at the ruins of ancient Greece. You look at pictures of Babylon or Nineveh and you find it has all been done before. You get people wanting to build up.

When I went to Brasilia, I found it was the same old thing: "Let's build the greatest city there has ever been." It has all been done before; there is nothing new: big buildings and impressive gardens, trees, pools. The fact that it has all been done before aggravated Solomon. When he had finished all his public works he knew he had simply repeated something and done nothing original.

The second thing that aggravated him enormously was that he was going to have to leave it all, just having got it finished. You know, I thought of this when I stood and we looked at the remains of Herod's palace at Masada, a remarkable construction. He died within six years of completing that palace, so he only enjoyed his summer holidays there for six years and it was all gone.

I think of Paul Getty collecting his treasures and building a Roman villa in California to house them and he was never able to even see them. He died before he could go and look at the incredible Roman villa that was built for him there. Solomon said, "I've got to leave it. What's the point of building up such a magnificent metropolis, if I have to say goodbye to it not long after I have built it?" This was the brute fact that stuck in Solomon's throat. It is a fact that would stick in anyone's throat if they stopped to think about it. The brute fact of death comes as the great leveller.

This was Solomon's great aggravation. He knew it is

better to be wise than foolish and better to have light than walk in darkness; better to see where you are going than not see where you are going. But where are you going? Six feet down. Since the wise and foolish die the same way and since the wise and foolish are equally forgotten, what is the point? One poet, James Shirley (1596–1666), wrote:

> Death lays his icy hand on kings:
> Sceptre and Crown
> Must tumble down,
> And in the dust be equal made
> With the poor crookèd scythe and spade.

Those words went through my mind as I stood in Bladon and looked at Winston Churchill's tomb. There it was, just one tomb surrounded by a lot of others, and the other names meant nothing. He was joining the unknowns. His name will survive a bit longer but already to my children the name did not suggest much, though it does to me. It becomes just a name, rapidly becoming part of dull, boring history lessons.

Solomon first had this dreadful thought that everything he had done had been done before. Second, there was this awful thought that he was going to leave it all behind and death would come as the great robber to him.

Somebody was trying to comfort Sir Walter Scott on his deathbed and said, "You will be remembered after you've been gone."

He said: "Posthumous reputation, the veriest bubble, with which the devil did ever delude a wretched mortal." Posthumous reputation a bubble – he uses the exact word that Ecclesiastes uses of life. Fame is very short-lived.

The third thing that aggravated Solomon was this: somebody else would get what he left who had done nothing for it. Because he said: "Who knows whether the man who comes after me and gets it all will be wise or foolish?" In fact, his fears were proved true because his son, Rehoboam, got it. He wasted it and he lost ten-twelfths of it almost immediately because ten of the twelve tribes revolted and set up independently in the north. He was only left with Benjamin and Judah in the south, and he wasted and lost it all. The kingdom that had been united for three reigns – those of Saul, David, and Solomon – was never united again and his son just lost it. From then on it was downhill all the way until it disappeared altogether. This was his worry: "I've built all this up and who will come after me and who will look after it?" Even if he is wise and not foolish, even if he looks after it, will it do him any good without working for it?

I remember talking to a wealthy man and he told me that his father had worked up from nothing and become very wealthy. His father had three sons and that father one day called his three sons into his room and said to them: "I want you to know now I have left you nothing in my will because I want you to get your money the same way I did. I believe that is the best thing I can do for you as your father." All three achieved what their father achieved. It takes a big father to do that, doesn't it? What love; what discernment.

Solomon though: that is what gets me; I have built it all up; I have accrued all of this, then I have to leave it. That is nothing original. Somebody who has never done a thing for it will get it and he may be wise, he may be foolish. Even if he is wise it will do him no good to have all of this to start with. Solomon had had most of it to start with and it had done him no good, so he was aggravated by that thought.

The cost of his search was frightful. He came to the conclusion – it is a strong phrase, but he said: "I hated life. It has played too many tricks on me. It is so full of promises, but none of the promises came true." That is about as low as a man can get. But it isn't the last word because, in fact, he did not do the logical thing which might have been to end his life. He did not do what Socrates did. The man of great knowledge, Socrates, finally drank the hemlock. He drank poison with his students gathered around him; he discoursed all that he had learned on life and then he drank the poison and died. Now why didn't Solomon do that? I'll tell you why: because he knew that there was a God and that God had given him life and it was not his place to take it from God. There must be a meaning to life even if the picture is not on the jigsaw box lid; God has the picture and that means there must be a meaning.

He believed in God – he was a Jew and he knew that there must be meaning somewhere. As a philosopher, the writer of this book has to teach people something positive. If life is useless, if life is chasing the wind, if the road of enlightenment and the road of enjoyment, and the road of enrichment lead to nowhere, then how do you cope with life? What do you make of it if you don't know the meaning and you don't know the "Why?"

Well, he comes out with some very practical advice. It is amazing that so strong are the illusions that he mentions, people still try those three roads. But Solomon advises something rather different, namely: if you really want to make the most of life, the one that comes nearest is *enjoyment*. The problem was that he expected too much from enjoyment, more than it could give him. Therefore, his advice is: be modest in what you demand of life. Accept anything good that God gives you and enjoy it – simple pleasures like eating and drinking. Enjoy what you have earned but don't expect too much from life. He tried to get more out of life than it could give him. He tried to squeeze it dry.

That was the most positive advice he could give and frankly if we didn't have the New Testament, that would be the most positive advice I could give you. That is: don't kill yourself trying to get knowledge, don't kill yourself trying to get pleasure, don't kill yourself trying to get rich; but be content rather than covetous. Be content rather than clever and enjoy what God gives you. Now that is not bad advice for a start. It doesn't take you all the way, it doesn't make life worth living, it doesn't answer all the questions, but it is a good start. I can tell you that from experience, having lived among poor people as well as rich people; having been in some of the wealthiest houses in the land and some of the poorest, and having begun my ministry among the simple fishermen in the Shetland Islands, I know that some of those simple people, in a two-room croft with a soil floor, were happier than most of the faces on a London tube train. They were happier because they were not trying to kill themselves to try to get clever or to get rich or to taste every pleasure. They thanked the Lord for what they had. A contented person with little is better than an ambitious person trying to get a lot. Is that beginning to speak to your heart? There is something called the "rat race". What Solomon is saying here is: get out of the rat race; don't kill yourself for any of those things but accept what God gives you and enjoy it. Remember that you cannot decide whether you get to enjoy life; God decides that. So if he decides to give you something to enjoy, then enjoy it. Don't kill yourself to try to get more of it. Now that is very sensible advice based on his observation and experience.

This is "under the sun". If your thinking is confined to what the world can offer you under the sun and within this life before you die, then that is the very finest that you can do. Outside of Christ, I could take you to people in England who are living contented, happy lives because they are doing precisely this.

But that is not the whole of the answer – it leaves me still unsatisfied. It leaves me at the end of life saying, "This has been not a profit but a loss." Sir Walter Scott also said this, "I shall never see the three score and ten and shall be summed up at a discount. No help for it and no matter either." That is not satisfactory, is it?

There is more to be said. Jesus said, "What shall it profit a man if he gains the whole world and loses his life?" The prophet Isaiah said, "Why do you spend your money for that which does not satisfy?" Yet we do.

We turn gladly, thankfully and eagerly to the New Testament because there we find something more. I have a bit of Humphrey Davy's diary (the man who invented the safety lamp for miners). After he had written in his diary, "I am very miserable," he tried to find a remedy for his misery and this is what that great scientist said: "I envy no quality of mind or intellect in others. Not genius, power, wit or fancy. But if I could choose that which would be most delightful and I believe most useful to me, I should prefer a firm religious belief to every other blessing. For it makes life a discipline of goodness, creates new hopes when all earthly hopes vanish, and throws over the decay, the destruction of existence, the most gorgeous of all lights calling up the most delightful visions where the sensual and sceptic view only gloom, decay, and annihilation." What a quote! There comes a point where a clever man says, "The thing that would be most useful to me now would be a religious belief."

Let me tell you now what the New Testament offers. The first passage that comes to my mind vividly is Romans 8. If the question is "God, why did you make life this impossible jigsaw?" the answer is that God made it impossible for us to find meaning to life without him – that is why he did it. He put us in a world where nothing fits until he fits. He puts us in a hollow world where nothing fills until he fills. He puts us in a crooked world where nothing gets straight until he straightens it. He did it for our benefit and for our sake so that we might seek him. As St. Augustine famously put it: "Lord, you have made us for yourself and our hearts can find no rest until they find their rest in you."

That is why he did it and that is why your life is a jigsaw you can never make up until you find God. It was God who subjected the whole creation to futility in hope. Isn't that little phrase extraordinary? There is something in people that makes us different from every other animal. We reach out for the answer, we reach out for the meaning, and we want to make sense of life. My dog isn't a philosopher; my dog never asks these questions. My dog is thankful for any scraps thrown after dinner, and is fairly contented with that. But men ask questions and they say: what is the picture on the jigsaw? What is the pattern? What is the meaning? What is it all for and what is the point?

People rise above creation—they are in futility, and in hope. They are always searching for the answer and always using the old roads and not learning from previous generations that they are all dead ends. But they go on because there is hope, there is futility and hope, and God made it that way so that you can never find life until you find him; until he straightens your crooked life out, and until he fills the hollow and supplies the missing pieces to the jigsaw and then they all fit together; the links come.

Man is so desperate to find the missing link between man and the monkeys but he can't be bothered to find the missing link between God and the meaning of life – though it is there to be found. It is only when you reach above the sun and say, "There must be a heaven, there must be a God, there must be a meaning and I'm going to reach for it by faith" that you begin to piece the jigsaw together.

Did you notice the key word from the readings in Ecclesiastes? It occurs 28 times. The word is "I". The subject of sentences in Ecclesiastes is "I" or "me". The real reason why these roads are dead ends is simply that they put self in the middle and self on the throne and say, "I will be enlightened, I will enjoy myself, I will be enriched, I will enrich the world." "I" is a dead end.

I turn to my Lord Jesus, who says: "What shall it profit a man if he gains the whole world and forfeits his soul?" and, "Lay not up for yourself treasures on earth where moth and rust corrupt and thieves break through and steal...." Jesus also says: seek first his kingdom and his righteousness and all these things will be thrown in as a bonus. There you have the secret. There is nothing morally wrong with enlightenment, enjoyment or enrichment. They only become wrong if they get first place because self gets first place. But if God has first place, all of these other things should come in second, third or fourth place and they fit in beautifully. A Christian is not an ascetic. A Christian is not someone who denies himself the pleasures of life. A Christian is not someone who says, "I am not interested in education"; a Christian is not someone who says, "I am not interested in making money." I know Christians who have said: "I am going to make as much as I can properly and morally and I am going to use it to enrich this world. I am going to use it for God." What is wrong with this ambition? Nothing at all.

I read this remarkable statement in a minister's diary: "I can truly say that while I become daily more convinced of the empty and unsubstantial nature of all earthly possessions and enjoyments, I find all the innocent pleasures and accommodations of life doubled and tripled to me." Do you understand that? The more he became convinced of the passing nature of the pleasures of this world, the more he enjoyed them. In other words, once you get this world into true perspective, you can enjoy it properly without becoming a slave of it. You can take everything that God gives you, and he gives us all things freely to enjoy. You don't feel that death is going to rob you out of the biggest thing in your life because death is taking you into the presence of God who is preparing more things for you to enjoy.

You see, you have got to get life in perspective. Rank things in the priority they should have. Get God in the centre and him on the throne, and then you can enjoy everything else that he gives. You don't live for the gifts then, you live for the Giver, but the gifts are enjoyed. That is a more positive philosophy. Solomon just says, "Enjoy what God gives" – that is all he can say. The New Testament shows us that we can enjoy God and we will then enjoy everything else that he gives us. Get right with God.

As I thought this through further I thought of Luke 15, the prodigal son, and how he tried one of Solomon's roads. Why didn't he read Ecclesiastes before he wasted his money and went to the far country? When he came home he found the very thing he had gone looking for: music and dancing and making merry. Isn't it ironic? It had all been "I" and "me". "Give me the money that is coming to me." When he came to his senses he said: There is more bread in my father's house for the lowest slave then I've got here among the pigs. He found out the hard way.

A passage that finally came to me with great force, interestingly enough came through another teacher in Israel, in John chapter 3. One night a scholar, a teacher, a professor – a man looked up to for his great insight and discernment – came to Jesus. He saw that Jesus had what he, Nicodemus, did not have. What was the secret? Jesus taught him the secret: You will have to start life all over again; go right back to the beginning – begin as a little child; get born again. Nicodemus wanted to know how. Jesus encouraged him to catch the wind. They were sitting on a rooftop, it was dark, and the wind was blowing through the Judean hills. To paraphrase the teaching of Jesus: "Do you feel that wind? You don't know where it's coming from and you don't know where it is going." It is like that to be born again. You can't explain what is happening but you feel it and you know that the wind of God's Spirit is blowing. Just reach out a hand of faith and catch it and start life all over again. Don't devote your life to things that lead nowhere; let God be at the centre.

We see something that Solomon could not see. Solomon said, "I was King in Jerusalem; King of Israel; my kingdom" – and that was all he could see. Once you have caught the wind of the Holy Spirit and you have been born again, what do you see? You see the kingdom of God. Now you have got something worth working for; not your own kingdom, which will be left to others who may wreck it and waste it, but a kingdom that will last for ever. You see your place in the life of that kingdom, as a citizen of that kingdom, with gifts to build that kingdom up. You have been born again and you can see the kingdom of God. You don't build up a little kingdom of your own. You don't want to be king any more; you don't fantasise: "Supposing I was king...."

A Christian lives the life of the kingdom of God and that makes life so full of meaning and purpose. Everything I do is worthwhile now. It all starts when you feel the wind of God's Spirit and you can understand what is happening. You may feel that you are coming to a fork in the road, to a crisis. You may begin to feel the following: God is real; God is speaking to me. I cannot predict how this will happen to you because I cannot predict the wind. It may come to you while you are reading or walking down the high street or riding in a tube train. The wind blows and Jesus says, "Catch it."

Just say yes to Jesus Christ. Say, "I don't understand everything about you; I don't understand what you're doing; I don't understand where it's going to lead me; but I know that if I don't grasp this opportunity I am going to miss life;

eternal life, real life."

It is not a new start in life that we need, it is a new life to start with. It is only the Spirit who can give new life. Those who really know what life is about are those who have caught the wind; they have felt their sails blow out. Now life isn't a rowing boat, it is like a yacht. They are being carried by an invisible power greater than their own, the power of the Spirit of the Lord Jesus who is alive today.

Read Ecclesiastes 3:1–15

I began reading this passage in a strange place – sitting on the Thames Embankment just outside Lambeth Palace, having got there a bit too early for an appointment. I glanced up at Big Ben, read "a time for war and a time for peace" and remembered eleven o'clock on a Sunday morning, 3rd September, 1939 when Big Ben said it was a time for war. It struck again all through the war: at the time for the nine o'clock news. Then it struck again when it was time for peace. Little had I realised then that time was running out for Big Ben. Experts from the atomic research establishment examined it because its main frame was showing metal fatigue, as were the hour chiming mechanisms in one or two other parts; so even Big Ben doesn't keep on going forever without maintenance. There will come a time when your clock stops too. There was a time when your birth struck, and your death will strike. The hour will come and you cannot alter that fact.

We have this very precious commodity of time. We may have different salaries, but we all have twenty-four hours a day to spend. What we do with it determines the kind of people we become and the type of future we have. Indeed, what we do with time decides where we spend eternity.

So it is a very important subject we have here. You will have heard this passage so often: a time for this, a time for that, and a time for the other, and I wonder what you have made of it. Some common interpretations of this passage miss the truth. There is an interpretation that puts all the emphasis on the fact that it is within your human capacity to decide the appropriate time to do something – so really it is saying there is a time and a place for everything and you should decide yourself. What is the appropriate time to dance and what is the appropriate time to kiss and what is the appropriate time not to do either of those things? That is virtually just saying there is a time and a place for everything. That is humanist philosophy and it would not be in the Word of God if that were all it was saying. The trouble is that most English translations gave the wrong impression by saying "a time" whereas the Good News Bible rightly says "the time". It is not "a time" and the message that will come through is that it is not your choice to choose the time; it is already chosen. But that would swing us to the opposite extreme and there are those who have interpreted this passage in a spirit of fatalism – meaning there is nothing you can do about it, your diary is absolutely set. Absolute predestination determines whether you will have marmalade or jam tomorrow morning. Every bit of your Monday morning is already mapped out to the last detail and you are to accept this more or less cheerfully, but as an act of sheer fatalism. The times have been so fixed that there is nothing you can do about it.

We find if we study this passage carefully that it teaches neither that it is your choice to choose what time you dance and what time you cry; nor do you have to accept in a fatalistic way like the Muslim. The truth in fact lies right between those two extreme views. What the philosopher is trying to teach us is how to respond to the tides of time; how to weave out of them a tapestry that has beauty in it, and purpose and sense.

For that is what this book is all about. As I mentioned earlier, the main questions this man is asking are: "Is life worth living?" and "What is the point of living?" – questions that many don't even bother to ask. But these really are the most important ones to ask because if you don't ask them you will waste your time. Or, at very best, you will pass it away. You can only use your time if you learn what life is all about – if you can get the thread of life; if you can respond to the tides that ebb and flow in joy and sorrow, and respond to them in such a way that you can grasp them and weave them into the tapestry. That is what this man set out to do.

We have seen that he tried to do it through getting money, through getting education, and through getting more and more pleasures in life, whether wine, women or song. He was trying to find the best way to use his time. He knew that he only had one life to live. The sadness and poignancy of this book is that it is written by an old man who said: I went through all those experiences without ever discovering the answer, and therefore I now plead with you young people, remember your Creator while you are still young because you will never get your youth again; you will never get your life back again and you must find out what your life is all about, what the point of it is, unless you are going to look back over a wasted life consisting of years that have gone without being well lived.

Some older people reading this now would give anything to be able to go back and be a teenager again because now they have discovered what life is all about, and they can't do it. So pay attention to an old man as he talks, as he muses back on the rich pattern of his life – on the contrast, on the light and the shade, on the times when he has danced and the times when he hasn't; the times when he has laughed and the times when he has cried; the times when he has attended marriages and the times when he has attended funerals. He is looking back and thinking: what was the pattern? Who called the tune? Who set the time? Who wrote my diary for me? What was the point of all that time spent, and what have I got to show for it at the end? Or his favourite question, which comes again in this passage: what profit does a man have at the end of the day when he lines the books off and adds up all that he put into that time and all that he got out of it? Or what has he still got left when time ceases to be for him? All that time spent. Because, you see, you can not only spend a lot of money and have nothing to show for it, as the prodigal did in the far country. The prodigal also spent a lot of time and had nothing to show for it. You have been spending time today and yesterday and last week and last month and last year. Ecclesiastes poses the question: what profit do you have to show for all that or was it time down the drain?

Instead of saying, "There is a time to be born and a time to die," the Good News Bible says: God sets the time to be born and the time to die. The time for sorrow, the time for joy—he sets the time. Whatever you may put in your diary, God sets the calendar of your life and the seasons of your life and there is not one person who can write in your diary even one month ahead that you are going to have a time of great joy or dancing or happiness on a certain day one month ahead. You may find yourself attending a family funeral. You cannot set the times. Yet what you do with the times that God sets is going to determine whether your life has point or not.

So it is a balance – God sets the times but what you do with the times he sets is your responsibility; how you respond to the tide. Indeed, it is the secret of life to be able to respond to the tide. That is the secret of good business; a person who realises double-glazing is going to be everyone's desire and he has seen the tide and he grabs it. Or a person who knows when certain stocks are going to go up; he or she senses the tide and responds to it. The individual doesn't set it but rather senses the tide and responds to it.

The secret of success in evangelism is also to sense when God's Spirit is preparing a situation and to get in there and exploit it. It is sensing the tide, catching the tide. "There is a tide in the affairs of men which taken at the flood...", said Shakespeare. That is saying what Ecclesiastes is saying. God sets the time but if you respond to it and seize that time.... In other words, if you don't spend all your life wanting to dance and to laugh and to be happy and to build, but if you seize those times of sorrow and mourning and loss and respond to them rightly, you can weave the whole lot into a life that is not pointless but jammed with purpose. That is the message and it is a message that is very relevant to us.

This man is a very honest writer; he paints a picture of life as it really is. He asks: what does man spend his time on? He comes to two conclusions: one, that life is full of contrast; and, two, that it is full of continuity. On the one hand there seem to be seasons which alternate with each other, and yet, on the other hand, there is a sameness about everything because it just comes back again. This is so true to life – your life is made up of contrast, moments when you have been deliriously happy and moments when you have been really down in the dumps. So there is contrast there, and yet somehow the contrasts keep recurring so that life is a series of ups and downs. Is that not true? That is life as it is, and God has set life as it is.

Now I want to make a few comments about the contrast, the ebb and flow of human experience, the rhythm of life. One of the reasons this poem appeals so deeply is that it is so true to our own feelings. It touches something quite profound. We know this is true, this rhythm of sorrow and joy, this rhythm of birth and death. So that even today there have been people dying and people being born and the rhythm is part of life. It is true – there are seven verses, which for the Hebrew is the perfect number. It is something akin to Shakespeare's Seven Ages of Man or Lawrence of Arabia's Seven Pillars of Wisdom – a phrase he pinched from the book of Proverbs. Somehow the number seven seems complete.

So this writer says seven times: look at the contrasts of life. In each of those seven verses there are usually two contrasts. Even poetically, it is beautifully constructed. But in the contrast, one is a welcome thing and the other is always a distasteful thing. One is something that we have all the time and the other is something that we try to keep out of our lives most of the time. Yet however hard we try to have this and not that, life becomes a contrast, an ebb and flow; life becomes a mixture. You have had your good years and your bad years, haven't you? You didn't plan that. You said: "I never thought I'd be in this situation this year", and last year you didn't think you would be in that one. Yet the tide of life ebbs and flows.

I want you to notice that he is conscious that we like the nice things and we don't like the horrid things. So he starts with the nice things and then when he gets to the end he reverses and finishes with a nice thing. Have you noticed? Just so he starts and finishes with you, and does not lose you. He starts with a time for birth – that is a time to be thrilled and happy and congratulate – then a time for death. Now if he followed through with that pattern, he would finish with "A time for peace and a time for war." But he realises that people don't like being left with war so he reverses and he finishes with a good thing, a time for peace – "Shalom". You know, if you take the first and the last word that is what we hope life will be. We hope that it will begin with birth and continue and end with peace, but it doesn't. We hope we will always be happy, but we are not. We hope we won't have to mourn but we do, and so life goes on.

Now he covers many aspects of common life: agriculture – a time for planting and a time for reaping; building—a time for demolition and a time for erecting. He covers sex. That phrase about casting and gathering stone, in other versions is just a euphemism for having sex. He says there is a time for it and a time not for it. He covers money – and there is a time to buy and a time to sell. He is covering the whole of life.

But he begins and ends with the biggest two facts of life. First, the biggest individual facts are birth and death. Second, the biggest social facts are war and peace. As I look back over life, it is safe to say now that those two couplets cover my life. I don't know the day of my death but I know the day of my birth. But the other huge divisions in my life are the divisions between peace and war. I am old enough to remember the period between 1939 and 1945; the period of rationing, the period of crouching in an Anderson shelter and listening to the sound of bombs. So my life has been divided into: peace, war, peace. My life started with birth and it will end with death. I have tasted quite a few of the other things in between. This is life as it is – one contrast after another. Yet these contrasts seem to keep on coming so there is continuity and a sameness about everything.

Years ago there was a series of television programmes on the "Life of a Village" which simply eavesdropped on the things that happened in a village for twelve months. A television critic commenting on an episode – which covered egg-rolling down the hill and a local parish election with all the inevitable tensions between people that arises in a rural life in that situation – commented that it was varied enough, yet satisfying instead of bitty, because the theme was there, all the events being facets of one fact of rural life: nothing lasts forever but nothing is totally destroyed. Now that is what Ecclesiastes is saying here: nothing lasts forever but nothing is totally destroyed. People are born and people die, and yet it all goes on just the same way. Now that is the pattern of life.

We now turn to the second question: considering the power of life, who calls the tune? Who decides the seasons?

Who decides that next year at this time I will be wonderfully happy or that next year at this time I will be terribly sad? Who decides? There are only certain possibilities. Is it chance or choice? I mean by that: either the seasons are purely arbitrary impersonal forces beyond anyone's control, or someone is controlling them. Now you have to decide right now which of those is your answer to life – which philosophy you are going to live by. It is comparatively easy to say, "I live by the philosophy that it is sheer chance; it is luck; in fact, we are at the mercy of forces that have no feelings towards us." One of the religions in this country is astrology, which is simply fatalism. It is saying: "What happens to me at the supermarket today, meeting that tall, dark stranger, is the result of being born under a particular constellation and a particular arrangement of the heavenly bodies – it is forces that decide." You would be amazed at how many people believe that we are at the mercy of impersonal forces of chance and that it is simply a matter of good luck or bad luck. I will give you some of the phrases that illustrate someone who believes this: "Oh, I suppose it's just one of those things." Have you ever noticed some people talking like that? "I'll have to bear it because it's just one of those things." Here is a life dominated by "those things" – whatever "those things" are. So if sadness comes, it is just one of those things; nobody could do anything about it; I couldn't do anything about it. I am at the mercy of those forces.

Do you know, RAF pilots used to be like this? We were in a pretty active field where I was chaplain and something like half our pilots lost their lives in six months. This was in peace time so-called, but in the operations at that time that was what was happening. I talked to those pilots as their chaplain and said, "Do you know that you may be the one who does not come back tonight? I may be conducting a military funeral in a few days for you."

Do you know what they said? Invariably, to a man, they said, "Look it's like this. If your number is on the plane that day, that's it. There is nothing you can do about it, your number's up. I'd rather be flying a jet even if my number is on it today than sitting on my backside in an office pushing a pen."

Some of those men who were so brainy, so rational that they could control a highly technical machine, would never take off without a rabbit's foot; another thing that could somehow control another's fate! Here were highly intelligent men in the twentieth century flying these highly technical machines and they were saying: "Just one of those things; if your number is on the plane that day you've had it. If your number is on that bullet you will get it. If your number is up, it's up." Now that is an answer that the Bible will have nothing to do with.

The Hebrew word for luck is "gad". That is why the phrase "by gad" is something a Christian never says. You never hear Christians at the door saying "best of luck". Have you ever heard someone say that at a church door? We do not believe that the seasons are set by blind, impersonal forces of fate.

There are some who say: "It is my choice. I am the captain of my fate, I am the master of my soul. I will decide to be happy, I will decide to dance. I will defy fate. I will choose, I will fix my diary. I am in charge of my life." That is to be a fool – I say that advisedly. Jesus told us not to call someone a "fool" lightly but he called a fool someone who would say: "I've got enough money to retire well." Jesus said: Tonight your soul will be required of you. Then there are those who say their fate is fixed by others, and they always have someone to blame for the bad things that happen. Have you noticed that? It is always the government in power at the moment that has caused it all.

Who sets the seasons? Some people say: "I do; I choose."

Some people say, "They do", and "they" are to blame if we have sorrow instead of joy and mourning instead of dancing. But this book comes out very clearly with the answer: God sets the times. He sets the seasons. It is God who will decide when you die. It is God who decides whether next week will be a good one or a bad one for you. It is God who moves circumstances so that those circumstances exalt you or humble you. It is God who makes you rich or poor. It is he who brings that marriage into your family or that funeral. How you respond to God's calendar is going to be the secret to whether you find a real point to your life.

Now that is Ecclesiastes's answer to the question as to the power of life. It is not in your power or mine to control the seasons. It is not in the power of any "fate" to control the seasons. It is God who sets the clock; it is God who sets the time for your circumstances. It is quite an act of faith to believe this. Therefore, if I can say this, that means there must be a purpose because God is not purposeless. If he gives me an unhappy week this week, then there must be a reason for that. It is an act of faith to believe that God sets the seasons. Fatalism says: "There's nothing I can do about it except put up with it." Faith says: "What is God saying to me by setting this season?"

This is not predestination in its total form of forcing me to do a thing. Perhaps I might put it like this: When winter arrives, it gets cold – I can defy that and I can go out in my swimming trunks in the middle of winter; I can join those poor people at the Serpentine on Boxing Day and I can plunge into the icy water. I am free to defy the seasons. I might be a bit eccentric if I did so, but I am free to do so. What is predestined is that winter comes. How I respond to that, whether I co-operate with it or rebel against it, is the area of human freedom.

So God sets the time to mourn and you can laugh it off

if you wish. God sets the time when you can respond and repent, and you can harden your heart and walk out without doing so. God sets the season when you can rejoice. You can say, "I'm not going to dance, I am not going to be happy. Let the young people shout 'Hallelujah'." God will not force you to go with the times, but a person is wise who moves with the times which God sets – that is the message here.

Someone is wise who, when God sends a summer, enjoys it to the full and sunbathes in God's goodness, but who, when God sends a winter, says: "God, I praise you for this also because you want to do something with me." Someone is wise who, when he is a picture of health and is enjoying being alive and breathing, says, "Praise God I am well and I enjoy it!" It is also wise, when sickness comes, to say: "God, what are you saying to me?"

We move on thirdly, and finally, to the purpose of life, and again we see the sheer honesty of this man. Ecclesiastes is honest enough to say: I have searched all my life and I cannot see the point. I have not found the thread, I have not found the pattern; I have not found the purpose. Therefore, I have had to come to terms with my life and all its contrasts and I have come to certain conclusions. Conclusion number one: that God gives us the good and the bad and that both are beautiful. Now that is a big conclusion. He must be weaving a beautiful picture.

As I read this chapter I got a vivid picture in my mind of a gigantic tapestry frame and a lot of human beings on the wrong side of the tapestry watching bits of pattern come through. Sometimes they were black threads; sometimes they were white. Sometimes they were beautiful colours and sometimes they were dull grey. I seemed to see all these little human beings taking bits of thread and trying to crochet them into patterns and only getting a little bit done and then dropping dead. In my vision I walked to the other side and

I saw God, and he was pushing the threads through. On his side there was the most beautiful picture. All those odd bits of thread, dark and light, beautiful and toneless, were all weaving into a picture from his side. Those little bits of crocheting and knitting that those humans were doing on the wrong side meant nothing, and his picture meant everything and it was beautiful.

I realised that the man who wrote Ecclesiastes stayed one side of that tapestry and he never got round the other side, but he believed that the other side existed. That is the difference between the unbeliever and the believer facing life. The unbeliever says: "I will enjoy what I can. I will grab what I can. I will eat, drink, and be merry."

The believer says, "I will enjoy what I can, and when God sends something good, I will praise him because it is his gift. But, I will praise him for the other things as well because I believe that on his side there is the most beautiful picture being formed."

You see the atheist or the agnostic has to cope with the contrasts in a vacuum. The believer can trust that there is a beautiful picture. So the believer looks at the times when he has been very sad, the times when he has mourned, the times when that which has been built up has then been torn down, and he says: "Praise God – that is a part of a beautiful picture on his side and he wove it in." Doesn't that give you a different outlook on life?

I would be telling you a lie if I were to say: "I promise you, if you become a Christian, a life that is full of dancing; he will turn your mourning into dancing every morning and he will enable you to go through life without any more problems; it is just great being a Christian. Since I became a Christian everything in the garden has been lovely." I would be telling you a downright lie. But if I can lead you to a faith that says: "Even in those bad things that God has set the time for, he knew what he was doing and he was weaving a most beautiful picture which you can see" – how would you feel about that?

In the Old Testament, you cannot see this picture. That is why this book is essentially a pessimistic book. So how did he cope with life? He said: "You have set eternity in man's mind and yet you prevented men from grasping the meaning of life." What he means is this: you have given us a desire to make a picture of these times and experiences but you will never let us come around and look at it from your side; you have given us a desire to know the whole sum meaning and not just the experience of the parts but you never tell us, you never give us an understanding of what your overall purpose is and what the whole picture is like.

It is us looking at a gigantic painting with a tiny magnifying glass and we just see little bits and we wonder what it is. In the New Testament, God reveals what he is doing.

How did Ecclesiastes cope with this? The writer comes to the conclusion that there are two things you need in life: first, you need to have fun and enjoy the good things that God does give; second, you need to fear the God who is weaving out of the other things a beautiful picture for himself.

Those are two remarkable things, and to get them together is unusual. To find a person who has fun and fears God is unusual. Yet this writer says that is how he copes with life. When he gets the good things he enjoys them; he praises God and says these are God's gifts. But when he does not have the good things, that does not mean he has lost the purpose of life. These good things only become bad when you make them the point of life, the purpose of life. They are not the purpose of life; they are only part of life. The purpose is God's picture and so he is saying that when the bad times come he fears God because his work is so different to mine. When he does something it lasts forever; when I do something it is soon gone. When he does something it never needs correction or amendment; when I do something I always have to modify or amend it. When he does something he doesn't mind doing something he has done before. Yet I am a slave to novelty.

When God makes his tapestry, it is a permanent thing. It will last forever. Modern art won't. When God makes the tapestry of life he never says, "Oh, I must pull that bit out, I should have put another colour in there." He makes it perfectly; it never needs altering; it never needs adding to; it never needs taking from, says Ecclesiastes. When God makes his tapestry, he puts things into it as old as the hills. Birth and death are as old as the hills and he weaves them into the tapestry. He is not striving for novelty as we are. He is taking things that are very old and is making them into a beautiful tapestry.

Now that is as far as Ecclesiastes could get and if that were as far as I could take you I would leave you disappointed. I would leave you saying, "You must spend the rest of your life on the wrong side of the tapestry. Since you cannot see the picture and therefore do not understand what it's all about, enjoy the good things, have fun, remember that they are a gift from God, and have fear of God and remember that the bad things are a part of his picture even if you can't see it" – and that would be all I could say.

But, praise God, after I studied this chapter I turned to my New Testament and the passages that take me around to the other side of the tapestry or picture. I turned to Ephesians chapter 1 and this is what I read: In all his wisdom and insight, God did what he had purposed, and made known to us the secret plan he had already decided to complete by means of Christ. This plan, which God will complete when the time is right, is to bring all creation together; everything in heaven and on earth, with Christ as head.

The secret has been told; I now know what God is doing with my life. I now know why he sets the seasons. Everything has got to be summed up in Christ – that is his purpose. You will see this when you get into Christ and when you become a Christian and see the picture that this old world isn't going through cycles; it isn't just seasons repeating, it is a line that has a beginning and an end. The end is that one day there should be a Christian universe.

The mind boggles when you realise that is the secret design. Do you get the thrill of it – a Christian universe? We talk about Christian England. It isn't Christian; there isn't one nation in the world that is Christian. It is the first time we will have a Christian nation – when Christ comes back and the Jews return to him.

For the first time we will have a Christian nation then. But could you imagine a Christian earth? Could you imagine a Christian moon, Christian stars? That is God's tapestry and he is fitting it together, and that is the grand cosmic purpose that God is working out. We only see the bits of it that he sets as times in our life. The time of your birth and the time of your death God set to be part of his tapestry.

What a concept. It is then that you can begin to say some very confident things. It is only as you respond to Jesus Christ that you can begin to say this: I am absolutely certain; I know that all things work together for the good of those who love God and are called according to his purpose. I now know that the dancing and the mourning, planting and reaping – every experience that is set for me by God – is going to work for good and be part of a most beautiful picture, and life is beautiful.

Whatever experiences come to you, whatever God's times are that are set for you, you can say "my times are in your hand". That is a lovely phrase now, isn't it? Whatever I put in my diary, it is what God puts in my diary that is important. Even though it may not be welcomed, it is now beautiful. All things are brought into Christ and I can suffer in Christ as well as dance in Christ. Life has become a whole; a beautiful thing.

That phrase "my times are in your hand" comes from Psalm 31, just a few verses after another verse which says: "Into your hands I commit my spirit." Who said that? Jesus, a young man of thirty-three, said that. A young man whose life was being cut off by wicked men; a young man in his prime who had done nothing but good for people and who is God. Jesus had only been in public life for three short years. People could say, "Oh, what a waste, what a tragedy." But from the Psalm that said "my times are in your hand" came those words, and: "It is finished."

Though Jesus had not travelled beyond a little part of the earth's surface and though he had written no books and though he had not met many people outside his own nation, he had fulfilled the most beautiful and perfect picture of life there has ever been. In three short years, he had responded to the times, which the Father had set. Earlier, when they had tried to kill him he had said, "My time has not yet come."

He knew what time it was – he knew when it was the time to rejoice and make merry with his friends, and they called him a glutton and a wine bibber. He knew when God the Father had set the time to go to Jerusalem and to die. He always knew what time it was – not by his watch, for he didn't possess one. Nor, as far as I know, did he have a diary but he always knew what time it was—have you noticed that? He knew whether it was a time to rejoice or a time to be sad.

When they criticised him for going to parties, he said that it was not the time then to fast, not the time to be sad. There would come a time when that was right. He knew when it was a time to wreck and a time to build. Some people's lives he took apart and some people he built up. He knew when it was a time for war and when it was a time for peace, and his times were perfectly in the hands of the Father. So when he came to the end of it, even though he had only done three years of public work and he was only thirty-three, he said: "Father, into your hands I commit my spirit." His times were in the Father's hands. It was time to die.

Isn't that beautiful? There are people in their sixties and seventies who are not ready to die; who feel that they have made such a mess of life and wasted so many years, they would like to hang on a bit more to make something of it. Not Jesus. He knew the time and it was time to go home. He had known the time and had done everything that the Father wanted him to do. You see, that is all the time that you have got, you haven't got any time to spare. You have one life; you can only live it once. It is just long enough to do everything that God wants you to do. He has set the times; it is too short to waste any of it.

So I plead with you, whether you are young or old: do you realise what time it is? For some it is high time to seek the Lord. For some it is time to consider full-time Christian service. For some it is time to fall in love and get married. For some it is time to give your affection and attention to other things. For some it is time to dance, for some it is time to mourn. But you don't need to be a fatalist; you need faith.

My times are in your hands, God. Whatever this week brings, I will call it beautiful – because you have set it.

Read Ecclesiastes 3:16–4:12

From this point to the end of chapter six in the book of Ecclesiastes we have pretty depressing reading. Here is a man with neither blinkers nor rose-coloured spectacles, who looks squarely at life as it really is. He is very observant. He looks at society and writes it off. He says it is full of injustice. Unless you really close your eyes to the facts, you must agree with him that the world today is no better than the world he describes here.

As little children, one of the first phrases we learn when we begin to string words together is: "It isn't fair." Have you ever heard a child say that? They say nothing but that at a certain stage. We have this deep sense of injustice from our very early years. As we grow up and face life as it is, it grows. Have you noticed it always works upwards, never downwards? We always feel more keenly how unfair life is when we compare ourselves with those who are better off. It is very rare that we are as moved or as anxious to square the situation up with those who are worse off than ourselves. By nature we envy those above us. Injustice is even more difficult to bear when it appears in places where you would expect justice. I have sat in a court in a country (that I am not going to name) where bribery and corruption is the order of the day, even in the legal world. I have sat in a place where we expected justice but instead saw injustice in the very law courts of the land. Somehow injustice hurts more deeply when it comes in the very place where justice should be most clearly seen. Law courts may represent one

63

example; government circles can be another. Surely if a government is anything it ought to stand for justice. When injustice appears at the government level, it is more difficult to bear because these are the people you look to, to equal things out – to make things fair and just. A lot of injustice or sense of injustice lies behind political turmoil.

This is the scene on which the writer of this book looked when he said: everywhere I look I see injustice; life doesn't seem to be fair from beginning to end. He noticed what Psalm 73 describes – that life in this world does not work out with the good being rewarded and the evil being punished here. Saints suffer and sinners escape. Many wicked people die in peace in their beds after spending money and time on themselves all their lives. Many really lovely people seem to go through one traumatic buffeting after another as they pass through their earthly pilgrimage.

This deep sense of injustice – life doesn't fit our faith. We believe in a God who is good. We believe in a God who is loving. Then why does life work so unjustly? Why do the innocent suffer and the guilty go scot free? Why can a criminal sell his life story for thousands of pounds to the Sunday newspapers? It doesn't seem right or fair.

This man came to the conclusion that life was a jungle. It is very interesting that that word "jungle" came to be increasingly used about human society in the twentieth century. People were saying more and more: "We are simply naked apes." That is not true. The human skin has more hair follicles (about half a million) than any ape. Nevertheless, the parallel is being drawn all the time and we used to get phrases as the "blackboard jungle" applied to schools. We had phrases such as "the concrete jungle" applied to our great metropolitan areas. The message going around was that life is a jungle and the law of the jungle seems to prevail. This was Charles Darwin's worst contribution to human thinking.

There is an extraordinary trail from Charles Darwin's book *On the Origin of Species* right through to Nazi Germany and to Russia and to China. The trail lies through the word "struggle".

Many came to believe that man is simply an animal in the struggle for survival – the struggle for existence. You can trace the word "struggle" through the philosophers like Nietzsche through to a corporal from World War I writing a book in prison: *Mein Kampf* (*My Struggle*). You can trace it right through from Darwin to Marx who talked about the struggle between the proletariat and the rest – the struggle for existence – and this word "struggle" became the key word and you can trace it right through into twentieth-century politics, science and philosophy. It is riddling our thoughts with an idea that life is simply a jungle and therefore we just fight each other and in the process many have to die. The biggest fact of life in a jungle is that there is death occurring every minute, all the time; it is one species preying on another. The weakest go to the wall and the fittest survive.

It was that theory, that outlook, which went straight from Darwin into Nietzsche to Hitler and plunged us into World War II: let the fittest race survive and let the weak go to the wall and let the old and decrepit go to the euthanasia clinic and let the Jews go to the gas chambers – this was the whole philosophy. It does seem that life is like this: millions die every decade through one form of injustice or another. Every day thousands of people die of hunger. It seems so unfair, so unjust, and it goes on.

So the philosopher tried to grapple with this fact in relationship to belief in God: God, why do you let it happen? What are you trying to say? What are you trying to teach us? He came to a very unusual conclusion. It is presented to us as his conclusion, not as God's answer to the question, but it is interesting to see his conclusion. He came to the conclusion that God let it happen to show us quite clearly that we are no better than animals; to bring us down from our pinnacles of pride and strip off the veneer of our social development and strip away all our ideas of progress and show us that underneath we are beasts; we are brutes and we treat each other worse than the apes treat each other.

As Richard Wurmbrand said: "To say that we are descended from the apes is an insult to the apes. No apes have done to each other what we human beings have done to each other." Now on modern planet earth the cruelties are perpetuated. I do not think there is any experience more shattering than when I take the parties in Israel to the museum of remembrance of World War II. It is all we can do to get people together into the bus after that because somebody in the party is wandering off, almost in a state of shell-shock.

To see what men can do to little children and the cruelty and unfairness of the world in which we live: "God, we are just animals" – that was his conclusion. God, is that what you are saying to us in letting it all happen? Are you saying we are just animals? Well, God, you are right because we both come to death. Here he sees death as a reminder of our creatureliness. Oh, we think we are so big, so powerful, so great, and we finish up in a little box six feet down. In fact, if you look at the rotting corpse of a human and the rotting corpse of an animal, there is no scientific observation or evidence to show that anything different has happened between the two. They both come from dust, in that every particle of my body is the same as the chemicals to be found on the crust of the earth and we both go right back there. This body that I am using will one day take its place again on the dust of the earth. So I finish up the same way my dog does. For all our greatness, for all our achievements, for all our human glory, the greatest finish dead as the animals do. It is at this point that this man writing within the framework which I described as "under the sun and within this life" can see no evidence that there is anything beyond the grave. So he has to come to the conclusion that this is basically an unjust world and that we must accept its injustice, and that the most we can make of that fact is, on the one hand, to see that God is teaching us that we are still animals in a jungle and no better; and, on the other hand, we are back to his advice of an earlier chapter to enjoy yourself while you can for there is no way to know what will happen after you die.

That is where the observant unbeliever must stand. I cannot see how the humanist can believe in justice in this world. I cannot see how the agnostic can believe that this is a moral universe because the evidence is all to the contrary. If I had no knowledge of anything beyond the grave, I think I would give up and I would say: "Well, the most I can say is that God is simply leaving us in the jungle." But it is an unjust world, it is an unfair world, and there is not much that we can do about it. Praise God that I will be able to tell you what it is like beyond the grave.

The area where science cannot go, the area where the historian cannot go, the area where no one can go – the area beyond the grave – lies beyond the power of human discovery. Everything we know about life after death comes to us by divine revelation, not by discovery. It is beyond our powers to penetrate that thick veil. So if we could not penetrate it in some way, if someone could not tell us what lies beyond, if there were no hope beyond the grave of injustice being put right, of things being restored to their proper order, of the good being rewarded and the evil being punished – if there were no possibility of that beyond the grave – then I think I would just give up. I couldn't live in such an unfair world if I knew that it was never going to get any better and could never be put right, for that is what is being pointed to here.

Ecclesiastes then goes a little further and says that not only is there corruption in the world, and suffering, but cruelty and oppression. It is not that some people just go hungry, it is that other people seem in a crazy way to enjoy causing suffering. It is a world in which power goes to people's heads. Or, as Lord Acton observed, power tends to corrupt and absolute power tends to corrupt absolutely. The oppression in the world cannot be relieved because the power lies with the oppressor. There is a vicious circle. If you have a rebellion to turn an oppressor out, what happens? Those who have started the rebellion become in turn corrupted by the power and in turn oppress.

This is true of every race on earth: those in power can oppress others because they have the power. I think the most vivid memory I have of that is watching the news reports of Hungary attempting to be free from the USSR. There was all the frustration as you saw men throwing stones at tanks. Why did we not go in? In 1939 we went in because Poland was being treated in that way. It was because the oppressor had the power and all we could do was watch helplessly on television and say, "Tut, tut. Isn't it dreadful," and go back to our tea.

The writer of Ecclesiastes looked at the condition of mankind and he got to the lowest point in his feelings as he looks at life in 4:2–3 where he touched rock bottom.

How do you feel about street attacks and robberies? How do you feel about that happening in England? The power is with the oppressor, so on its own little scale it is drawing ever nearer our world and our own experience.

The writer finally came to the conclusion that he envied those who were dead and gone. If I were not a Christian, and if my reading each day was only the news, I think I would envy those who are dead and gone. I don't think it will be long before we get to that stage. What a world we are moving into. Ecclesiastes goes even further: such a terrible world is the world that I observe – a world of oppression, a world of cruelty – in fact, those who have never been born are better off than those who have been dead and gone because they have never even seen this world. The best state, the most blessed state, is never to have opened your eyes on this scene at all. Can you sink lower than that? I don't think you can.

The second lowest point of oppression is to wish you were dead. I am sorry if you are finding this depressing, but the Bible knocks you down in order to pick you back up. It humbles us in order to exalt us; it makes us face life as it is in order that we may face life as God meant it to be and as God can indeed make it. So this is the lowest point in Ecclesiastes: the writer wishes he were dead; he wishes he had never been born; he wishes he had never seen it.

The next thing the writer looks at is the rat race. He is still forcing us to look at life. So far he is taking a kind of world picture, and injustice in the world is the most obvious fact that he has seen. If you study our world at all, that is the most obvious fact that you see. The gap between the "haves" and the "have nots" is widening daily, and it is so unfair. But now let us look more closely at the world of commerce, the world of "rat race". I find that phrase most significant. There are certain parts of the animal world where animals co-operate with each other. Have you ever watched ants? Isn't it fascinating to see how they co-operate together to do something? Or have you ever studied bees? They have got workers going out to get the honey. They have a fan of bees at the doorway to the hive keeping the air circulating. They have got the queen bee, and every bee is co-operating with the others to keep that hive going. But there are certain species in the animal world that do not co-operate, in which each individual is so concerned about itself that they will attack their own species, and such an animal is the rat. This is the origin of the phrase "the rat race". It is a picture of horrid, scurrying creatures, every one only concerned for its own survival and therefore prepared to jostle, to push, to attack, to bite – anything to survive – even to attack other rats.

This expression has come to be applied to trains full of commuters going up to London in the morning. The funny thing is that it has been a race that has been run for a very long time, and Ecclesiastes explains it perfectly. It is a world in which, first of all, there is competition and, second, addiction to things. There is competition to get them. Once you are into the rat race you become addicted to it so that you cannot get off it even if you want to. Even after there is no more reason to be in it, you stay in it because you are hooked.

Ecclesiastes looks first at the spirit of competition and puts its finger exactly on the motive – envy. The one thing we cannot stand is being outclassed by someone else. It is a feeling that can keep coming into our hearts. It is the most difficult one. It was one of the worst motives in history. It was responsible for the first murder in history. Cain killed Abel out of envy. It was responsible for the worst murder in history because for envy Pontius Pilate delivered Jesus up.

Christians are not immune to envy. People do not like others to get ahead of them. We call it "keeping up with the Joneses". It is phrased in many different ways, but there is a desire to have what others have, to be what others are, to do what others do. If the next-door neighbours are going overseas for holidays then we must. If they get a new car, then we must. It is the rat race and envy that puts us into this.

It is essentially wanting something that someone else has that gets us into the race. It is the urge to get on an "up". We would rather depress another person in their fortune and bring them down to our level than rejoice with them in being up there. I wonder just how much of this motive lies behind pressure – to be up with others – behind quarrels about wage differentials; always looking at someone who has a bigger salary and saying: "If they have it, why can't we?" That is the rat race.

With rare discernment, Ecclesiastes points us to the fact that the trouble is that the rat race produces the opposite by reaction. It produces the "dropout" and we are given a description of the lazy, indolent dropout who prides himself on not being in the rat race. The dropout folds his arms and is proud of not being in the rat race. In the most vivid Hebrew, Ecclesiastes says that such a man is eating himself up. Laziness is suicide – it is like cannibalism. A man will sell his own self-respect if he is no more than a dropout in the rat race. He chews himself until he loses his grasp of reality. He loses his desire and ambition to achieve anything in life. Laziness is one of the easiest ways of getting out of the reach of God, because God is very busy. He is a worker. When Jesus came, he said: "My Father works until now, and now I work." He told his followers: work while it is day; the night comes when no man can work. A dropout loses the opportunity of finding in work the meaning of life. He tries to find it in leisure and that is not where God has put it. God has put the meaning of your life in your work.

So between the person in the rat race working himself to death, and the lazy dropout, un-working himself to death, who is left? Ecclesiastes points out that there is a small group in the middle who are content, and here I give you the literal translation of the Hebrew: "who are content with a handful of quietness". That is a lovely expression. It means someone who has done a hard day's work but is quite content with what he has got in his hand at the end of the day – quite quiet about it, unlike the man who is grabbing with both hands everything he can in the rat race, and the dropout who has folded his arms and is doing nothing with his hands at all. The man who has done an honest day's work and is quietly

71

content with what he has earned, and has a handful of quietness – that man has discovered one of the secrets of life.

There is a profound truth. These people are few and far between. I don't meet many people who have a handful of quietness at the end of the week, but I do meet some. What lovely people they are. They seem somehow to be right, they seem to have discovered what life is about. They are not grabbing with both hands.

That leads Ecclesiastes on to a very positive note: partnership pays. As this man looks into a competitive society in which some grab and some drop out, he points to the truth that the person who really gets there is the one who has learned to co-operate rather than to compete. He has discovered that two can do more than one and three are more than two. It is a simple observation and a profound one. He is not talking about marriage, though I am sure I have used this at marriage services and I am quite sure you have heard it referred to in marriage. But he gives some simple examples of where you have co-operation rather than competition; togetherness rather than the loneliness of the man in the rat race or the loneliness of the dropout. Both are lonely people. Both are people who somehow lose their friends, even their families. The man in the rat race wakes up to somehow find he is estranged from his wife and his family and has drifted away from them. The dropout suddenly realises he has no colleagues and no real friends. Even those he mixed with are no longer there. But the man with the handful of quietness is the man who seems to get along with people; to regard them not as rival rats, but as friends, colleagues.

Take, first of all, co-operation between two. Two are better than one. It is not just that one plus one equals two, it is that one plus one equals five. Somehow, two people can do together what two separately cannot do. They don't add one person's efforts to another; they multiply it. There is something about two people doing something together that multiplies their effectiveness.

Here are three examples. First, they multiply their effectiveness in work; two people tackling a job together can do it better than one can. I remember on the farm how unrewarding it was to plant potatoes the hard way by yourself. You hang a sack around your neck and you bend your back at right angles and you cut two slits in either side of the sack with a knife. Then bending your back you go along the row and, alternately, you put your hand in and bring a potato out and drop it into a hole about nine inches to twelve inches from the next one. Believe me, when you are doing that by yourself you keep straightening up, getting so tired you can't go on. But if two of you are there, you just keep going, and five o'clock comes and then you straighten up. Two work far more effectively than one.

Another example of co-operation is this: if two of you are together and one falls, the other can help. Imagine mountaineering. Two individuals are climbing a mountain by themselves alone. One falls – there is nothing he can do. How do you climb a mountain? Why, you rope two together. Then if one does fall the other can hold, take up the slack and rescue that climber immediately. You will get to the top of the mountain much more effectively in a team roped together, even with one other roped to you, than if you tackle it by yourself. It is far safer.

Then this lovely illustration of two in a bed. An aunt of mine had a favourite phrase: "Like two spoons in a drawer." It is most descriptive. It is not of marriage, though it is certainly true in that sphere. You really need to see people in a tough situation to see this. Take, for example, Arctic explorers; you see them settle down for the night and you will see them as close together as possible. Or in the desert you see the Bedouin in Arabia. The desert night is so cold there can be keen frost from the burning heat of the day. The Bedouins, when they settle down at night, really get as close to each other as they can and thus reduce the area of heat loss for their bodies.

Do you remember a plane crash in the Andes that hit the headlines when they were reduced to eating the flesh of some of those who died? Apart from the flesh that they ate, which caused all their controversy, the main factor in their staying alive was the fact that they got so close together they managed just to keep each other warm enough. Right through life you can see that competition kills but co-operation brings life.

Why is it then that we seem to be such a competitive society, and so little co-operation seems to occur in industry and commerce? What can't we get it together? Why can't management sit down around the table and co-operate instead of competing in a "them and us" fashion? This is at the heart of the problem of life's injustices. If only we could co-operate instead of being competitive then the injustices could be dealt with. Do you see the line of thinking here?

Finally the writer caps it by saying "three are better than two". I drove over the Severn Bridge and looked again at that magnificent structure. I find it a fascinating piece of engineering, in particular the two great wire ropes that go up over those concrete columns. When you look closely at those wire ropes they are made up of tiny, individual strands. If you had watched that being built you would know there was a spinning wheel that went up and over, back again, over again and back again, over again, time and time again – like a spider weaving a web. It was laying each time one more strand and it was being twisted in and together into one rope. That wire rope, made up of individual strands together, can now hold all the traffic going between England and Wales.

Says Ecclesiastes: "Even three strands twisted together

you will find very hard to break," and three people really held together in a team, you will find very hard to break. Two are ten times better than one, but three are ten times better than two.

Let me now with joy come to the New Testament. So far we have been looking as far as any humanist might look at our society and we have come to one very simple conclusion: what we need is a world in which there is co-operation rather than competition; in which people work together instead of for themselves. Isn't that in a nutshell what this world needs? Could it be put more simply than that? I want to tell you first the bad news and then the good news. The bad news is quite simple: there is no hope of our world becoming a co-operative world. It will remain competitive until it disappears. I have no hope whatever of the humanist dream in a united human race removing injustice from the earth. The New Testament makes it quite clear that the human race will never become the two-fold and the three-fold cord.

But now for the good news: within the human race God has planted his Son, and he is starting a new humanity; a new race, a new man. Characteristics of this new humanity will be precisely co-operation instead of competition; liberation instead of oppression; contentment instead of covetousness; and, above all, togetherness instead of loneliness – and he is doing this right now between Christian believers – people who, with all the growing pains and all the tensions that belong to their old humanity, are nevertheless being formed into a co-operative body, into cords that cannot be broken, into a united family in which injustice is removed. It is being done as individuals become partners with Christ. The first twosome that is needed is for a man or woman to get together with Jesus and something begins to happen when they get together. When the man or woman falls, Jesus picks them up. They work effectively together, and then two become three and three become four. The most unlikely people who in other circumstances would have been competitive find themselves members of one body and co-operating to do something lovely for God, and a beautiful people is being formed. Now I am not unreal in this. I know many churches, warts and all. I know all the problems and the growing pains. Yet to me the exciting thing is that I see a society on earth that is not only dedicated to these ideals but is beginning to achieve them; a society in which people of all ethnic groups can love each other.

I see a society in which it is not a matter of competition, but in which if one rejoices all rejoice, and if one is honoured all are, and if one suffers, all suffer. I see a society that is bringing east and west into one family. I see a society in which people are being set free to be themselves and accepted as themselves. I see a society that is not a jungle but a garden. I see all that coming to be in Christ.

Therefore, I say with Ecclesiastes that the dead are better off: for me to die is gain. Not because you are out of it but because you are further into it. A Christian never says, "I wish I had never been born", but a Christian does say "I long to depart and be with Christ." Because he knows that you are not confined to live within that narrow box "under the sun" and this side of the grave.

The Christian has discovered that it is God's plan to scrap this world. He is going to have an almighty bonfire. He is going to burn the whole thing up and blow it up. Out of the ashes will rise a new heaven and a new earth in which righteousness and peace kiss each other; in which good dwells; in which people live together in harmony; in which the rat race and the dropout are things of the past; and in which together we shall serve him day and night in his temple. What a vision!

I pity the writer of Ecclesiastes that he was born at the

wrong time − before he could know all this. There are just hints in the Old Testament, but now we know that the thing which is most characteristic of the animals − death − has been conquered, and now we see man not like the animals but like the angels. We even see a new universe in which man will be above the angels. The human beings capable of being such brutes and beasts to each other become sons of God in glory.

If I did not have this hope I could not face the world as it is. I would have to live in the self-delusion of the humanist who believes that it is all getting better, but as I read Ecclesiastes, it says to me loud and clear: the world is no better now than it was in the year that he wrote that book. What is better is the incarnation of Jesus and the living hope to which we have been born anew by his resurrection from the dead and his promise to make us new creatures; to blend us together until we have all things in common − until we love one another as he has loved us; until we see that rivalry and competition has no place within the new humanity; until we see that injustice can be dealt with, but only when it is dealt with by love rather than might.

That is my vision and my dream is that this is going to come true. It is not a fantasy, it is an act of faith. It flies in the face of facts. This world as I see it is an unjust world and will never be any better, but into it already the kingdom has begun and already even its social effects are seen. Already, Christians are proclaiming the kingdom of God. It has arrived, you may enter it; you may live; you may be melted and moulded into this one new humanity in Christ Jesus and then you know that it is much warmer to be together − and that if you fall you will be picked up.

Notice that the Lord Jesus sent people out two by two. But in fact there were three because he was with them, and a three-fold cord cannot be snapped. Praise God then for this a man who climbs to the top of the political tree has only two things ahead of him and both are profoundly disturbing: the first is stagnation and the second is extinction.

That may sound cynical and there are many still clambering up the ladder who would disagree with him. They often come to the conclusion that he was right, but they come to that conclusion too late. Remember this was 2,500 years ago. He said: I can see that a man can come from the very bottom and get to the very top; he can be a totally unknown person. He can even come from prison and rule a country. If you count up the countries of which that has been true, you will be amazed. A man can come right from the bottom to the top, but what happens to him when he gets to the top? You can become, in the late President Nixon's term, an "exhausted volcano".

The writer can see someone who makes his way right to the top can become a person who will not listen to advice, who loses sensitivity, who loses touch with the people who helped him up there – and who becomes caught up in the corridors of power. So there is a getting out of touch and out of sympathy with the people, a kind of enclosed mentality which withdraws and becomes an anachronism. Somewhere in the multitude is a young man whom nobody knows who has got his eye on the same ladder and on toppling that man over and replacing him. It has been going on for hundreds of years. A man gets right to the top, stagnates, exhausts, does not listen to advice, gets out of touch, and very quickly there is another young man climbing the ladder behind him who says: off there, I want that place now. As soon as a man comes off the top, the next thing that awaits him is extinction. Ecclesiastes, with a rather poignant note, says that it won't be long before he is forgotten. A man may rule over a huge number of people, but when he is gone will they remember him with gratitude? How quickly human fame dissolves with time. There is a whole generation in Britain who just know Winston Churchill as a name, little more, and never feel a stirring of gratitude in their hearts. In fact all of us in the UK benefit from one man whose name is almost forgotten. Have you heard of William Beveridge? He it was who introduced the National Health scheme and National Insurance. How quickly you get to the top and how quickly you fall into obscurity. You think you are going to leave your mark on history and the mark is erased so soon.

In Ecclesiastes, having considered the palace, and having seen how men got to the top, and the stagnation and extinction that comes there, the writer is considering: if they get trapped up there, what happens to the people down at the bottom? He turns his attention from the top of the ladder to the bottom and he finds among the ordinary people a sense of deep frustration – first because they cannot get their rights. Somehow, the people at the top seem insensitive to the rights of others. The unemployed, the aged, those who have no house, and those who are handicapped and those who are least able to protect themselves, feel a sense of disillusionment. They promised us this, they promised us that, and we are not getting it.

Then comes the final note of disillusionment. Ecclesiastes reminds us that if this is what happens to people at the top, people at the bottom are frustrated because there is a sense that they will never get justice because they cannot break in. They cannot get wrongs put right. Why? Because each official has another official over him to protect him. That official has another to protect him and there will be a cover up, from the top to the bottom. There will be an attempt to cover up what should come out, and it can be found there in chapter 5.

This then is the Ecclesiastes view of life: there are people scrambling to the top, getting to the pinnacle, getting isolated there in their corridors of power and losing touch with the people who are increasingly frustrated and who feel that they cannot get through the hierarchy of bureaucracy to get wrongs righted and to get things out. Isn't this strange?

The disillusioned man walks up the hill from the palace to the temple. Do people behave any differently when they go into the house of God? He sees people hurrying to the temple and he wants to say: stop – watch your step when you go into the temple; I have been up there and what I have seen is disillusionment. What did he see? Two things. First of all, he saw ritual practices without any real meaning; secondly, he heard lots of rash promises that meant nothing. He might have thought he would only get that in politics, but he found it in religion too. Let us first consider the ritual practices. When he got into the temple he found people offering sacrifices to God. Oh yes, they were costly sacrifices, but when he looked into their hearts he realised that people were going through the motions of religion without the morality. They were going through the ritual without the righteousness. They were patronising God. They were more bothered with the cost of their sacrifice than the reason for it. They were more concerned with doing their bit by God and doing a favour to him than with fearing him. They were more concerned with what they did in the temple than with what God told them to do outside it – and he was disgusted.

One of the main dangers of religious practices is precisely that you go through the motions without asking God what he is saying. What is the sacrifice for? It is for sin. Ecclesiastes is a warning to be careful when you go to the house of God. Before you offer your bit, before you say, "I've given my contribution" have you listened to what God wanted to say to you?

For us, the main point of going to church is not what you have to give to God but what God has to say to you. It is an insult to patronise God and to think that attending his festivals and giving a contribution when the local church steeple is falling down is somehow doing your bit. God wants to talk to you about right and wrong. He wants you to listen.

The other thing he found in religion was rash promises. People were saying things that they never meant, and all of us are guilty of this. The road to hell is paved with good intentions, and the kind of religion that many of us have is the religion that says things to God and we intend to keep them and we don't – and God must be disgusted with us.

What promises have you made? Maybe it happened in an Anglican Confirmation service, or if you were married in church and you said: "... for better for worse, for richer for poorer, in sickness and in health, to love and to cherish, till death us do part...."

It meant: I am going to be loyal to the bitter end even if it is bitter, but I am going to be loyal. What happened to those words you said to God? Some have fought in a war and at the height of a battle have said: "God, if you'll get me out of this alive and bring me back to my wife and kids I'm your man for the rest of my life." Some have been desperately ill and going right through the crisis said: God, if you'll make me well and just give me back my health I'm going to be God's person for the rest of my life.

Ecclesiastes heard things being said and sung that he knew those people could not keep. If that is religion, then it is as hollow as a politician's promises to the country – if you just make promises to God and don't keep them.

There was a man in the church where I was previously pastor and he was a fine man, fifty years of age, chief accountant for an airline at that time. He used to come to church and stand during the hymns, his lips shut like a trap. His wife and sons sang around him but he stood there and never sang a word. Finally I said to him, "You know I'm amazed that you come to church. You never sing a word in a hymn. Why don't you?"

He replied, "Because I cannot mean it. I'm not going to sing anything to God I don't mean."

I was thrilled. I would rather someone came to church and didn't sing a word if they are as honest as that with God, realising that they are dealing with a God who keeps his word and expects us to keep ours. The kind of rash promises you make in the human sphere are totally out of place in the religious.

I will never forget one day I saw Reg open his mouth and he sang: "Take my life and let it be...." He sang, "Take my silver and my gold...."

Be careful what you say to God – Ecclesiastes teaches us that he might just take you up on it. He took Reg up on it and he told him to leave the house where he was and to move into a much larger house and to look after twenty-one elderly people. He gave up his job at London Airport and did that. He had said, "Take my life and let it be..." and God said: Right, I'll take it. The danger of praying is that God might answer your prayer. The danger of coming to a service of worship is that God might just take you at your word in the things you say. Oh how easy it is to say things in church. Somebody has called it verbal doodling. That is quite a phrase, isn't it? Playing around with God, trifling with a God who is a God of his word, who has never broken a single promise and who expects you to keep yours. The writer of Ecclesiastes discovered that the temple was "bugged" – every word that was said was recorded, and that one day there would be a day of reckoning and the recordings would be brought out. Do you realise that? God records all your prayers and all your praise, everything you say, even in a rash moment.

The one thing that would be needed to convince me that I needed to be saved would be to have a tape recording played back of everything I had said. I wouldn't need anything more, would you? That would damn me to hell. Indeed, not just everything I have said, but if God just played back to me everything I had ever said to him and then he said, "Now what about that? Did you mean that? Did you mean that? Did you mean that?" That would be enough to convict me as a man who was a liar. So Ecclesiastes looks at politics and he looks at religion and he finds both too full of words, too hollow, too empty, and he does not find life in either of those places.

Jesus, the Son of God, got to the top by going to the bottom. Here was the first man who had all the power in the universe in his hands and who was uncorrupted by it. Here was a man who never got out of touch with the ordinary person. Here was a man who was a friend of sinners, mixed with prostitutes, moved around the streets – a King and yet closer to his people than any other ruler has ever been. When they put him to death they stuck a notice above him: "King of the Jews". They did it as a sick joke. Yet there was one man, a dying criminal alongside him who believed Jesus, and he became the first citizen in Jesus' kingdom.

I have estimated that there are over one thousand million in the kingdom of Jesus, and that is growing every day. This one man has had the greatest influence of any because he is the Son of God. I just want to say this: one day, religion and politics will be totally merged – and with the best ruler there has been. One day Jesus Christ is going to be President of the United States and Prime Minister and King of England. He will rule over Moscow and Peking, for I am told in the Bible that all the kingdoms of the world are going to become the kingdoms of our Lord Jesus Christ. The government shall be upon his shoulder. Then and only then will you get a position where power does not corrupt and where the people feel that justice is theirs and oppression and frustration are bad dreams of the past. I am looking for, and longing for, the day when Jesus is king of all the earth. Are you not? When the government is on his shoulder – and his shoulders are big enough to stand it. Here at last we have a King who can reign in the right way.

I have got news for you: you don't need to wait until he is King of the world before you can come under his government. I am already under the best government there is and the best ruler there is, and his name is Jesus. Therefore, he brings me life that does not grow stale. He gives me ambitions that will not become hollow when they are achieved. He calls me to glory with him that will not go dead on me. He calls me to the only life that has got point and is worth living. Everything else is chasing the wind.

The writer of Ecclesiastes was a realist. He faced facts. The handicap he had was that he was born too soon. I thank God I was born after Jesus came.

Read Ecclesiastes 5:10 – 6:12

To read what Jesus had to say on the same subject, see Luke 16. I would say that mammon is probably the top religion of this country. Now the book of Ecclesiastes has reached the point where the writer takes a hard, cool look at the world's values. He has already said, "There's nothing new under the sun; nothing changes in this world of ours," and it doesn't. He could see that the society in which he lived was devoted to the god mammon (the god of money and that which it could buy) and that all around him were people who believed that if they could just get rich they would be happy. He looks very honestly at this assumption and he questions very seriously the world's values. Is it true that if you become rich you become happy? We live and act as if it is true. We are not prepared to let our standard of living go down.

Would we be better off if we were poorer or would we be worse off – that is the question which Ecclesiastes asks. The key word in this passage is "better". Who is better off? As soon as you ask that, the world answers: the person with more money, the person with a bigger wage, the person who retires earlier, the person who can buy this, that and the other is the one who is better off. The message of Ecclesiastes puts a big question mark against that.

One of the most disturbing articles I ever read traced back eight people who had won large sums of money. They had hoped to get rich to be happy and a reporter went back and said, "You got rich – are you happy?" Five out of the eight were desperately unhappy. The other three were still trying to cope with the situation but it really would put anyone off gambling. Someone might say: "Ah, but wouldn't I be happier if I had just that much more to buy those little extras that would make so much difference to life?" Would we? Who is better off in life – the person with money or the person without it?

There are five things that this passage says about money. First it talks about the disadvantages of amassing wealth. The New Testament says: "The love of money is the root of all kinds of evil." That was contracted into the title of a pop song many years ago as: "Money is the root of all evil" but that is not true. It is the *love* of money that is the root of all kinds of evil. Ecclesiastes begins to describe some of them. The first is that it acts like a drug. If I am hungry for food and I have some food, I am satisfied for the time being. If I am thirsty and I have a drink, I am satisfied. If I want money and I get some money I am unsatisfied. It is extraordinary but it operates this way – exactly like a drug where the more you have the more you need.

An ancient writer once said that if you could turn the whole planet earth into one round nugget of gold and drop it in the mouth of Everest, the mouth would just cry more loudly: give. Money has this extraordinary effect that the more you have the more you want and you do not become more satisfied or fulfilled. After a bit it begins to swallow your affections, your attentions, your ambitions, until you become its slave and you are possessed by possessions. I could take you to business tycoons, I could take you to compulsive gamblers, and I could show you the lives of men who have become slaves to that of which they intended to be master.

Not only does it become an addiction but it brings constant anxiety. Indeed, Ecclesiastes points out that a poor man may not have enough to eat but at least he gets a good night's sleep; and, "The more money you have the more mouths you are likely to have to feed." The more retainers you will have, the more people whose wages you will have to pay, the more insurance you will have to pay; the more responsibilities you carry, the more hangers-on.

I remember a man whose ambition it was to have a Rolls Royce. He wasn't too ambitious – he didn't want a new one. He was content with an old one but he thought he would love to say he had a Rolls Royce. One day he appeared at work in the Rolls Royce and people gathered around to see it. Though it was about twenty years old, nevertheless it was a Rolls. He sold it within twelve months. Do you know why he sold it? He couldn't afford to run it. Do you know why he couldn't afford to run it? It wasn't the petrol and it wasn't the insurance. It was because everywhere he went he was surrounded by outstretched palms. If he came into the garage there were some outstretched palms. If he pulled up at a hotel there was somebody with an outstretched palm. He was expected to tip and tip and tip again and he just could not live up to the image. The irony was that he was having to live up to his own prestige and he couldn't afford it, so he finally got rid of it.

Ecclesiastes could have told him that. You will get a lot of hangers-on as soon as you get money. In the New Testament we learn that when the prodigal went to the far country he found he had plenty of friends to help him spend it. (Actually, the literal Greek does not say that the rich man stays awake worrying but stays awake with indigestion – a kind of dyspeptic insomnia that attacks those in this condition.)

You have the absurdity in our society that a lot of money and effort is being spent to undo the damage that money and ease have done – the health clubs and the exercise machines for those who have got too fat. It is ironic that wealth brings some of these disadvantages.

I have seen so much tension in faces in London, compared with extremely impoverished places. Now please don't get me wrong, and please don't say that I am justifying poverty. I am just questioning the values of our society, as Ecclesiastes does, because Ecclesiastes has come to the conclusion that a poor man who has not had enough to eat, but is sleeping soundly, is better than a rich man suffering from indigestion.

With affluence comes indulgence that doesn't make us any healthier. On the contrary, it can have the opposite effect. The Bible is very practical. Did you ever think there were such practical things in it?

Secondly, the writer then moves from the disadvantages of wealth, which are pretty obvious, to the danger in acquiring it. Now the danger in acquiring it is simply stated: that you lose it while you are getting it. There are two major ways of losing your wealth. One is before you die and the other is when you die, and the book looks at both.

Here is a tragic situation. A man realises that he has got to deal to make money. (It is very rarely that you make a fortune by earning it; you usually make it by dealing.) He can be getting on so well and then make one bad deal and he has lost the lot and is right back to where he started, and he had seen it happen. Isn't it tragic when that happens? Here is someone who has been spoiled twice in his life: once in the gaining of wealth and second in the losing of it. He has had all that trouble for nothing and is right back to square one. He really hoped he was going to pull it off this time and it had precisely the opposite effect.

Of course, it can happen through no fault of the person. Circumstances just happen, so that someone loses all that they have gained. Ecclesiastes notes this. Isn't it dangerous to acquire wealth, because you can lose it so easily? Then it goes on to the very sombre and sober truth that you lose it anyway when you die.

A shroud has no pocket. Two people were discussing a wealthy man's decease and one said, "How much did he leave," and the other said, "Everything." This is the point at which everyone becomes a pauper. We go out of life as naked as we come into it.

Towards the end of his life, Dr Johnson built himself a superb villa at Twickenham and planted the gardens beautifully. He was showing the famous David Garrick around the gardens. As he did so, Dr Johnson said, "These are what make a deathbed so terrible." Isn't it tragic that men should give themselves to something they are going to lose? They may lose it before death, they will certainly lose it at death, and yet they have made this the biggest thing of their life – all for nothing, a chasing of the wind. There is only one worse thing than the addiction that money can bring. It is the emptiness that it leaves when it has gone.

The third thing that Ecclesiastes mentions now, and here it becomes more positive, is the delight in accepting wealth. This may come as a bit of a surprise to you after all we have seen in the book so far. There is a concern to help people to live with money – those who get it – to come to terms with it so they remain the master and never become the servant. There are two very practical things. First of all, as long as you see wealth as God's gift you will be able to live with it. You will be able to enjoy it. If you say "this is my achievement, this is my right", you will not be able to live with it and you will not be able to enjoy it.

Something happens as soon as you say: if I'm wealthy it is because God gave me the ability to get it; I also need the gift from him of the ability to enjoy it. If you have some money, if you receive an inheritance, if you are given some money, then say: it is God's gift and, if I enjoy it, that too is his gift. Then something else happens. As soon as you say that any money you have is God's gift, then the very next thing that you will do is to have in your heart a daily gratitude that does not rely on that gift staying with you in the future; that can enjoy having it today without worrying about losing it tomorrow; that can enjoy to the full what God has given now even if life is short and you know you are going to lose it all very soon.

That is very sound advice and I can tell you that I have met rich people who were not slaves of money, who did not worship mammon, who received their wealth as a gift of God and enjoyed it because God had given it, and thanked God for both the gift and the ability to enjoy it, and therefore they were the sort of people who, if it were taken from them, would say with Job very simply: "The Lord gave and the Lord has taken away, blessed be the name of the Lord." You cannot praise the Lord for the second thing unless you praise him for the first. It is only those who see everything that they have received as a gift of God who can say "Blessed be the name of the Lord" when he takes it back again. It was his so it is his to do with what he likes. If he takes it away then hallelujah that I had it for so long. But if he takes it away that is his business.

Job had a big argument with his wife when they went bankrupt. His wife said: "Curse God and die, look what he's done to you." She was really very annoyed at losing all that money and property. Of course, she was also heartbroken at losing the family. They lost everything, that couple – but the difference in their attitude was remarkable. The wife never said the Lord gave so she could not bless the Lord for taking away. She saw it as that which they worked for, which they had earned with the sweat of their brow. Job had built up the business. They had the family, had those children, built up the farm. It was theirs and now God had taken it all away. Job said, "Quiet woman. The Lord gave, the Lord has taken away, blessed be the name of the Lord." God had loaned it to them for that long; bless him for that.

That is Ecclesiastes' advice on how to eat and drink and to enjoy what you have while you have it, without becoming so enslaved to it that if it were taken from you, you would feel that life had dropped out. I think there is something quite wonderfully profound there. You can apply it not just to your money. You can apply it to your children, you can apply it to your relationships, you can apply it to your career, you can apply it to everything that God gives you and say: "God, thank you for it. I'll enjoy it while I have it; if you take it from me tomorrow I'll say, "Blessed be the name of the Lord for giving it to me yesterday" – what a different attitude. But the man who says, "I got my money. It was not God's gift. It was my right. It was my wage. It was my dealing that got it" will say: "God, why did you take it away?" has not come to terms with God's wealth.

The fourth thing that is mentioned in this passage is the difficulty in appreciating wealth. One of the most cruel twists of providence is that to some people God gives wealth without giving them also the ability to enjoy it. Sometimes it is because they are physically handicapped. Sometimes they are temperamentally handicapped. Sometimes they are no good at social relationships and so you find people incredibly wealthy who cannot form relationships. Some people have got everything that money can buy, and nothing that it can't. In fact, that was John D. Rockefeller's favourite phrase: "The poorest man I know is the man who has nothing but money."

Did you ever see the film *Citizen Kane*? There was something tragic about it. Here was a man who bought more and more things, who built bigger and bigger houses, finished up in a mansion, and he finished up a lonely, unhappy, miserable man. He got wealth and it was a gift of God, but he did not receive the gift to enjoy it. Ecclesiastes says that when you meet a man like that you feel it would be better to be a stillborn baby than to have lived that kind of life. You can see that happen to some people – the Ebenezer Scrooges of this world. They can even have a poor funeral with nobody attending.

At one of the saddest funerals I took there were, I think, only three or four of us at the service. The Will of the person when it was published ran into six figures. Of the three of us at that funeral, one had never known the person and was only there because they happened to represent a body that was the chief beneficiary. Somehow there was something awfully sad. There was so much money in this situation and so few people.

Ecclesiastes says: I would rather never have been born than have wealth and not be able to enjoy it; I would rather never have started life than go through the frustration of having all that money. Ecclesiastes reaches a very low point here and says of a stillborn baby – at least they go from oblivion to oblivion without the frustration of having money and not being able to enjoy it. It seems as if Ecclesiastes is saying there is no more futile and frustrating experience in life than to have the money and not be able to enjoy it yourself, and see strangers enjoying it because you somehow can't. There is something in you that prevents you from enjoying it. Job and Jeremiah both had this same experience where they got to the point and wished they had never been born, and envied a stillborn child.

So we come to the fifth and final point about wealth here: the dilemma in assessing wealth. Ecclesiastes is left with two major questions, which cannot be answered within the framework of present observation. The writer has looked at wealth, had seen that there is one way to live with it, and that is to accept it as a gift of God and enjoy it while you have it without being upset when you lose it. But the two simple questions left are these. First: who is better off? Secondly, what is best? The writer has tried to grope after the answer as to who is better off.

He did not have a clue as to who was best off. He writes: Who is better off? I don't know whether a rich man is better off or a poor man. I don't know whether a wise man is better off or a foolish man. The conclusion to which he came was that it is better to be a contented man than a covetous man – and that was as far as he could get. He had looked at people and had seen that happiness bears no relationship at all to wealth. What he saw is that a man with a little who is contented is better off than a man with a lot who is not. As someone has said: the richest man in the world is not the man who possesses much but the man who desires little.

In this debate about who is better off, you can do nothing about it because life is decided by God, and you cannot shape your life. You may decide to make a lot of money and you may achieve that, but you cannot decide that you will enjoy it.

So the reader is left with this huge question: who is best off? The answer in this book was that God knows. If people use that phrase today, they mean: I don't; no human being does. Ecclesiastes concludes that no human being knows who is best off; only God knows and he is not telling.

So from that point I turn to our Lord Jesus Christ. God became man, and he knows. So I have someone whom I can ask to tell me who is best off: Jesus, God who has become man, knows and he is telling. Jesus said more about money than about any other subject. Did you realise that? If you go through the Bible and underline every verse of Jesus' teaching that touches on money you will find that he said more about this than about prayer, heaven, forgiveness and any other spiritual subject. Money is all the way through his teaching because it is such a big factor in life.

He said that it is hard to be rich. You know, here he was

walking through life and almost everything he used he had borrowed. He had no home of his own. When he wanted a donkey he had to borrow that. He was put in a borrowed tomb at the end. He looked at life very squarely and taught his disciples that it is hard to be rich – very tough to live with money. He said it on an occasion when a rich young man found that it had not led to happiness, came to Jesus and asked about how to find real life.

Jesus gave him honest advice. The best thing the young man could do was to go and get rid of his money and then come back to Jesus. The man stared at Jesus and looked very unhappy. He was at a fork in the road. Was Jesus right? The young man had devoted every minute of his adult life up to that moment to making money because he was sure that was the way to life. Here was a man telling him he had been on the wrong track altogether and telling him to get rid of it. He could not bring himself to say that Jesus was right and he turned around and he walked away very sadly. Jesus saw that it was so hard for men like that.

Simon Peter, who was always opening his mouth and putting his foot in it, came right out with his thoughts. He wanted to know: if people with money can't get to heaven, who can? That showed he had the same outlook: that this is the key to everything. So Jesus had to tell him that a man's life does not consist in the abundance of his possessions. You must never measure the importance of a life by how much money has been made during that life. That is no measure at all.

What else did Jesus say? In Luke 16, Jesus told two stories. The first story was about a rich poor man, and the second was about a poor rich man, and he said it all. Christians have real problems with the first story. It is about a thoroughly dishonest man. He was going to lose his job. He was given a few days to get the accounts ready to be audited, and he knew that the books were cooked. He knew that his days were numbered and that he was going to go. So what did he do? He fiddled even more and he got people to rewrite the IOUs which he held in their writing. He got them to write them down and they were jolly grateful to him. They said, "That's great ... I only need to pay up half of what I was going to pay. Thank you so much, I will remember you for this," and that was precisely what he was doing it for.

The master in the story commended the unjust steward for acting shrewdly. Why was he shrewd? Because he realised that life consists of relationships, not money. He realised that what you need at the last is friends, not money. He was prepared even to fiddle the accounts to get some friends, so that when he had nothing left there would be people who would be grateful to him. Jesus is not commending fraud and he is not telling you to go and fiddle the books. What we learn is that we are to give away and use our money in the same way: use what God gives you to give you friends in the future, so that when you get to heaven there will be people who say, "I'm so glad to meet you. Your money is the reason why I'm here. I'm so glad."

You see, you cannot take your money with you to heaven but you can send a bit of it on in advance in the form of friends. You can use the mammon of unrighteousness to prepare a circle of friends who will welcome you into heaven (see Luke 16:9). In fact, Jesus' advice is not to lay it up on earth (where you are bound to have depreciation because moth and rust consume and thieves break through and steal and you cannot be sure of keeping it) but to lay up treasure in heaven. That means: put your money where your heart is. Indeed, where your money is, there will your heart be also. He taught people to invest wisely in that way.

That is the completion of Ecclesiastes. The man who finishes up with no money and lots of friends is best off.

Think of the person who so invests what God gives him that there are people waiting in heaven ready to say: "I have been longing to meet you because the money you gave bought a Bible which brought me to the Lord. The money you spent sent a missionary to tell me about the love of Jesus and I am so thrilled."

Now that is an attitude to money. Yes, it is a gift of God to be enjoyed, but also to be used for an investment for eternity. It is literally true that Jesus tells you how to keep it beyond the grave, how to spend it so that you don't finish up a pauper.

So he told that very disturbing story about the rich man and the poor man. The poor man would love to have had the bits of food that fell. In those days they didn't have table napkins. They would take a piece of bread and rub their hands on it to get their hands clean, and if you have ever made pastry as a child you know how quickly the dirt transfers from your hands to dough. So they rubbed their hands and then they would throw it under the table. It was the dirt from their hands rubbed on a piece of bread, and this beggar would just love to have reached out and taken that little bit of bread.

But as soon as they died the rich man had a very pompous funeral – a lot of ceremony. The crowds had turned out when this rich man was dying. His great funeral was the best funeral there ever was. Lazarus died and there was no funeral (there was none recorded) but he found himself at a feast with Abraham very quickly. The rich man realised what had happened. He said: "Please...." Here is this rich man who could have bought anything he wanted, and had done so, living in luxury, now asking for someone to bring a drop of water on their finger – asking for the beggar to come with a drop of water for him. How extraordinary the reversals that take place in the moment of death when the last become first and the first become last.

Now don't get me wrong, Lazarus didn't go to heaven because he was poor. His name means "Lover of God" because though he was poor he could have a good night's sleep – he loved God. There were dogs to come and lick his sores if nobody else would come and bandage them. This man loved God so the angels carried him.

"Send someone to my five brothers" There they were, devoted to making money, indulging themselves, and they were going to be paupers, begging for water.

"No, they have got the Bible, let them read it."

The Bible talks about money, the Bible tells you what to do with it. The Bible tells you its dangers. The Bible tells you how to delight in wealth if God gives it to you. The Bible tells you how to bless God if he takes it away. The Bible is a book about money.

"They have Moses and the prophets, let them listen."

"No, father Abraham, if somebody should rise from the dead they will believe."

Don't you believe it. If someone rose from the dead they would not alter their life one bit.

I finish by reminding you of one of the loveliest things that was ever said about Jesus. It is this: that Jesus was fabulously wealthy and became poor so that we through his poverty might become rich. Do you realise how wealthy Jesus was before he was born? All the glory in heaven was his; all the universe was made for him. It all belonged to him and he turned his back on all that and he was born in the filth of a courtyard where the animals were, and he was laid in a manger.

Now that is not a very nice thing to do and you would not lay your baby in a manger where animals had been slavering over their food. Then, through life, he walked the roads. He had no money. When he had to pay his taxes he had to tell Peter to go and fish for it because he hadn't got it to pay.

The early church was very much like that. They could say: "Silver and gold have I none but what I have I give you." That was the poverty of Jesus, and yet through his poverty we have become rich.

So I am thankful that Ecclesiastes questions the values of life; it poses this question: who is better off? – and who is best off? Thank you, Jesus, for answering that question.

Read Ecclesiastes 7:1–25

Ecclesiastes was asking the right questions about life and groping with all his energy and thought for the right answers. He was asking whether life was really worth living. What is it all about? Why am I here? Is there any point to life? Consider that famous phrase: "Vanity of vanities; everything is vanity." To translate that into modern English we have to say: "Life is pointless."

In the first half of Ecclesiastes we have an atmosphere of cynicism, disillusion, even despair. In chapter 7 the book begins to be more positive. It is concluded that a wise man is better off than a wealthy man – that is progress. It is a little halting step forward towards the answer, which he never found but which we have found in Jesus Christ. It is lovely to see someone starting from his own premises, from an observation of life as he sees it, starting from the utter integrity and honesty which very few people have, being prepared to admit that he had reached dead ends and that he was getting nowhere fast. Starting from there we see his first halting steps towards a better life.

We see man seeking to better himself, a man who is asking: "Who is better off?" You have probably seen the keyword in this passage: "It is better, it is better, it is better." Here is a man who is at least beginning to make some value judgments and beginning to say: That kind of life is better than this kind of life.

I can begin to tell you something positive. He does it by showering upon us a series of proverbs. Proverbs are wonderful. They are a way of distilling human experience into a pithy, picturesque phrase, which is so easily remembered that wisdom can be passed down through the generations.

God has sanctified this form of literature of proverb. Indeed there is a whole book in the Bible called the book of Proverbs, but there are proverbs all the way through. Jesus was always quoting them; Paul quotes them, and here are some right in the heart of Ecclesiastes. They are so picturesque; so memorable. Take the first as a marvellous example: "A good reputation is better than expensive perfume." Do you like that one? Do you understand what it is saying? It is saying that everybody wants to make a good impression on other people; everybody wants to be attractive; everybody wants to be popular. Now there is a quick way to make people like you, and that is to get expensive perfume and put it on yourself. The slower but better way is to have a good reputation. The world is trying to say: "If you want to be attractive then have a bath and all sorts of things happen after you have had a bath in this stuff." If you study advertising, you know that advertising is saying that the expensive perfume is the way to make yourself attractive, and the aftershave is the key to success.

This writer looks at life and is saying that if you really want other people to be drawn towards you, see that you have a good reputation. That is very profound wisdom in a sentence, and it deals with the lie in so much commercial advertising to which you are subjected. When did you last see an advertisement suggesting that you build up a good reputation so that other people would find you attractive? It is a pithy little proverb.

One commentator says that first proverb hardly prepares us for the body blow of the second: the day you die is better than the day you were born. No doubt you remember what your date of birth is. Have you ever thought about the year of your death? Have a rough guess what year you will die. Let us just assume you have got three score years and ten, then in what year are you going to die? You may be very reluctant to think about the day you die. It is a fact that we celebrate our birthdays but the last thing we want to do is to start calculating the day we die. I have done a few calculations. I am going to assume that my life is a day of twenty-four hours from midnight to midnight. Therefore what time of day is it for me? Here are the results. If you are eighteen years of age, it is six o'clock in the morning for you. If you are twenty-seven years of age, it is nine o'clock in the morning. If you are thirty-six, you are at noon. If you are forty-five, it is already three o'clock in the afternoon. If you are sixty, it is eight o'clock in the evening. Do you find that disturbing? Ecclesiastes suggests that is the sort of thinking that does you good, but it's the sort of thinking that the world runs right away from. There was a saintly Christian who used to sleep with a skull by his bed and he did it because the Bible says it is better for you to think about the day you will die than the day you were born.

Why? It is because birth is so welcomed to us, such a lovely event, that birth is surrounded by fantasy and fancy. A baby is born and we all lean over the pram and say, "Goo-goo," and it is all a dream world. We don't stop to think that that baby is going to die. We don't stop to think that that baby has been born a sinner. We don't stop to think of all the trouble that life is going to get into. We live in a kind of euphoria – what a sweet little baby – as if it is this perfect life that has come into the world. We are so thrilled. Birth never teaches you to ask the right questions – but think about your death. Go into a funeral house and you think about the right questions. You ask the right questions of life. If birth leads people into a cloud cuckoo land of fantasy, it is death that leads them into the real world of fact. The greatest fact of life is death and you are a fool, says this book, if you don't think about it. Indeed, it says: "Sorrow is better for you than laughter and a man who is always thinking about happiness is a fool." Would you agree with that statement? Jesus taught exactly the same truths, and that sorrow is a good deal better for you than happiness. Or we could put it another way: is it not true that prosperity reveals your vices and adversity brings out your virtues?

Is it not also true that people are more likely to pray at a funeral than at a party? Is it not true that festivals are designed to stop you thinking and crowd your mind with so many thoughts that you do not ask the right questions, whereas a funeral brings such thought with it that it is so often drowned with a tea afterwards. I have talked to people after funerals and the last thing they want to discuss is the day of their death. The sooner they get on with the ham sandwiches the better they get away from the reminder, and even death itself is dressed up. I come from the north of England where until quite recently it was the custom for little children to be lifted up to see grandpa in his coffin. In the south I noticed we whisk the remains away out of sight – something not quite nice. Death has become the great unmentionable subject. In the Victorian age sex was the un-talked of thing and now death is. That is the second group of proverbs.

One of the great puzzles I have in life, and it began very early with me as a child, is this: why are the things that are good for you things that you don't like and things that are bad for you things that you enjoy? Have you had that problem? The quickest way to put your child off eating something is to say, "It's good for you." Their immediate reaction is, "Then there must be something bad tasting about it and I'm not going to eat it." But as has been pointed out, there are many sweet things in this world that are poison and there are many bad tasting things that are medicine. Here is a man who has lived long enough to decide the difference.

The third group of proverbs he throws at us concerns fools and wise men. He says: keep out of the company of fools; there is flattery there, there is fun there, but neither do you any good.

It is much better to have a wise man tell you that there is something wrong with you than to have a fool flatter you – but which do we prefer?

I don't know if you have ever lit a bonfire and put thorns on it. If you have, you will know what he means. Thorns blaze up quickly and they pop. Each thorn is like a bubble that expands and pops, and it cracks. It blazes up, cracks, and within minutes it has gone. You don't get a lasting fire with thorns. The writer says: "That's the laughter of fools. They blaze up, they cackle away in their laughter, and it's gone." You don't get any permanent warmth in that kind of fellowship. It is like cocktail party laughter – hollow laughter that is so quickly gone. Keep out of the company of fools. There is flattery and fun there, but the fun is so fading and the flattery will do you more harm than good.

This writer has seen that someone who takes a bribe or pays one pays a terrible price for that. The price he pays is that he has sold himself. He has sold his integrity for that bribe, and that is too big a price to pay. You are selling your character for that hard cash. Ecclesiastes makes it clear that it is better to have character than cash.

Finally the passage moves on to life's injuries and insults and makes the very sound point that it is better to be a patient person than a proud person because a proud person gets hurt and angry. There are two forms of anger – you either blow up and it comes out or else it goes in and becomes a grudge and a resentment. The writer can see that pride is behind both temper and grudges. He said: it is better to be patient than proud. Of course it is, but how? Ecclesiastes tells us what is better – it can tell us that it is better to be long-suffering and let insults go over you than either to give them back with interest immediately in a fit of temper or to harbour a grudge.

Now do you see anything in common between all these proverbs? They seem a real mixture up to now, don't they? What is the thread that ties them all together? There is one theme behind every one of these proverbs, ranging as they do from perfume to death to bribery. The thread that draws them all together is that wisdom is living for the future rather than the present. To put it another way: a wise person always considers the long-term consequences rather than the short term. A man who takes a bribe is living for the present, not the future. He is better off in the present but he is going to be worse off in the future, and he is living on a short term. A wise person is someone who takes a longer look at life; a silly person is one who lives for the present.

I would call it the Esau syndrome. Of Jacob and Esau, one lived for the long term and one lived for the short term. The man of faith is the man who lives for the long term. Esau comes home and he says, "I'm famished; I want a plate of soup now. I don't care what you ask me for and I don't care what I barter for it. Give me some soup now" – the original existentialist living for the now. Jacob says: "Fine, you can have my soup, I would just like your birthright when dad dies" – and Esau handed it over. What a silly fool. When the time came, Jacob got the money, not Esau. It was all over a plate of soup. Yet if you laugh at Esau or if you consider him to be a fool, how many fools are there even now exchanging eternal glory for a night's television? What fools people are if they live on such a short-term basis.

So a good reputation is better than expensive perfume. Why? Because expensive perfume lasts you twenty-four hours; a good reputation will last you a lifetime. The day you die is better than the day you are born because if you think about death that will give you a long perspective and it is only when you come to die that you really see life in its true evaluation. It is only then, from the light of the grave, that you look back and you really see what has been worthwhile and what has been a silly waste. So all of it is: take the long-term view. If I were to take a bribe and be fifty pounds richer today, ten years from now I would be a much poorer man because I have sold my integrity. Take the long view.

Of course he could not take a long enough view. He could only see as far as the end of this life and that is not a long enough view to be wise. That is why he never finally got further than these proverbs. But now we hear people talk about the "good old days", and that can be foolish. Such thinking can become a substitute both for action and for thought. You may be looking back with rose-coloured spectacles, only remembering the nice bits. The good old days were not always good old days – we just think of them that way. A wise person lives for the future and says, "What is going to be the result of this in the long term?"

As we shall see when we come to Ecclesiastes 12, the time to prepare for old age is during your teens. How many teenagers do that? Did you do it? Remember your Creator in the days of your youth. Get ready now for your old age. That is going to be the message later to young people, but will they listen? Take the long-term view. You can see straightaway that, as soon as you do, you change your habits. For example, you see at once that smoking is silly and brushing your teeth is sensible – as soon as you take a long-term view. If I take the short-term view, I don't see a need to brush my teeth and I can smoke as much as I like; take the long-term view and the whole situation is reversed. It is taking the long-term view that is so wise and so rare, and that is what he is saying.

So that is why he says that the end of a thing is better than its beginning. The ultimate outcome is the better guide than the original start. It is not whether you have started something but how you finish that matters. Any athlete will tell you that, and anybody who has done anything worthwhile will tell you that it is not how you start off, it is how you finish. It is not your birthday you should be thinking about but your death day. That is going to put life in true perspective for you.

Having given us these examples of wisdom, we move on to a brief evaluation of wisdom. Just how much can wisdom do for you if you manage to find it? It is said, for example, that it is better than an inheritance. Would you think that? Would you rather receive a thousand pounds or a piece of good advice? In fact, wisdom is better than an inheritance. There is a greater security – you will be safer in your old age if you are wise than if you are rich. Would the world agree with that evaluation? It is said that it is better for controlling circumstance – wisdom can do more than ten rulers for a city. I have lived long enough to know that is true.

But there are certain drawbacks to wisdom and we have to face them now. The first limitation to what wisdom can do for you is that God still has the last word over your arrangements. You need to think about this: that you have got all your plans straight in front of you and God makes it crooked.

Ecclesiastes teaches us to be wise to plan for the future – but remember that God can alter all that. Providence has the last word. You can prepare for the future but you can't plan it. It is wise to say, "If I do this I am more likely to be better in my old age" – but remember that your old age may not turn out as you have planned.

God makes a thing straight and who can make it crooked? God makes a thing crooked – who can make it straight? Remember that even in all your wisdom you do not know what will happen next. It is important to realise there is this limit on wisdom. You can prepare for as many eventualities as you can see, you can think through to the ultimate outcome of your present behaviour, but you cannot *decide*, because God plans your future. So wisdom cannot do everything. The second limitation is this, and here is a passage which I am sure you wondered about, and wondered why God put it in the Bible: "Don't be too good or too wise, why kill yourself? Don't be too wicked or too foolish either, why die before you have to? Avoid both extremes and if you are religious you will be successful anyway." What did you think about that? I know people who jump on that text who may not know any other, but they say: "That's how I live. It's in the book. It's in the Word of God," and they shut their eyes to everything else the book says. The book says: Be holy for I am holy; and be perfect for your heavenly Father is perfect. But there are people who ignore all that and seize on this passage.

This is the attitude of the ordinary man who has not yet realised that life goes on beyond the grave. This is the natural, normal human wisdom that only sees this life, and the reason why he gives this rather extraordinary advice is very sound. He means this: As I observe life I can see that it doesn't pay to be good; I've seen a man who really tried so hard to be good and he died young and he died painfully; and I've seen a man who was bad and he lived on and he died peacefully in his old age. So it honestly is not worth it to try to be too good. Don't kill yourself being good because you might die anyway.

If the furthest you can see is the grave then that is very sensible advice and I can understand the ordinary man in the street saying, "That's my philosophy." Try to be good but not too good. Don't go to extremes, don't get religious mania, and don't be too bad because you are likely to get in trouble with the police. Just try to go down the middle and add a little spice of religion to keep you out of trouble and you will be successful anyway. That is worldly wisdom but as soon as I look beyond the grave that kind of advice is nonsense. You see, the writer is working within the parameters, within the limits of his observation under the sun before the grave – for who knows what happens afterwards.

Well, I will tell you. God knows what happens afterwards and God has said that if you are going to get through afterwards then the standard is perfection. You will never get to heaven on the advice in the passage. The writer is giving advice for those who are simply coping with this life and it is reasonable advice. It is saying: Don't try to be over-good because you might not reach old age anyway; life seems to be very arbitrary. It is reasonable advice but as soon as life beyond the grave opens up, then this advice becomes obsolete. It is not wisdom, it is foolish and this was his limitation.

There are two more limitations on wisdom. First, don't expect to be right all the time. Everybody makes mistakes. However wise you are, don't take yourself too seriously. Finally, don't become hypersensitive to criticism. If you are too influenced by other people's comments then you will soon be a nervous wreck. You will soon be deeply hurt. Why? Because you know you have said wounding things about others which were not true. You have tried to vent your spleen against them by making a criticism. They are doing it about you too, so just don't listen to them too seriously. If someone were to listen too seriously to everything everybody else said about him, he would never get anywhere.

So it is wise not to go around digging up what everybody says about you. Pascal the philosopher said, "If everybody knew what each said of the other there wouldn't be four friends left in the world," and this is very sound advice. Don't go around digging up what other people say about you because they are just doing to you what you have done to them and you need not take it too seriously. This is all good common sense stuff but where is it getting us? I am afraid I am left at the end with the disappointment that he felt, and I offer this paraphrase of his thoughts here:

In my useless, pointless life, I have seen everything; I devoted myself; I was determined to get wisdom. I studied it. I wanted to find out how silly sin is. I tried to find out wisdom and foolishness. I found a few things that are better than other things. In the last analysis I have been unable to plumb the depths of wisdom. I have not found it, my search has not led me to wisdom. I still don't know. I believe that wisdom is the secret. I believe that this is the right path but I can only go a tiny little step down this path. I can tell you that it is better to have a good reputation than expensive perfume, but that is as far as I can take you. I can tell you that it is better to think about your death than about your birth, but that is as far as I can take you. I can tell you not to take too seriously what other people say about you but I can't take you any further. I have searched and I have not found, it is too deep.

There is something rather sad about this. All he can do is give us a little homespun advice about not going to extremes, not trying to be too religious.

Where, then, is wisdom to be found? I will tell you where it is to be found. It is yet another illustration of the fact that the Old Testament is utterly incomplete without the New. Consider some words of wisdom almost identical to the ones we have been studying, but try to spot the difference.

Jesus looked at his disciples and said, "Happy are you poor, the kingdom of God is yours. Happy are you who are hungry now, you will be filled. Happy are you who weep now, for you will laugh. Happy are you when people hate you, reject you, insult you, and say that you are evil because of the Son of man. Be glad when that happens and dance for joy because a great reward is kept for you in heaven for their ancestors did the very same things to the prophets.

"But how terrible for you who are rich now, you have had your easy life. How terrible for you who are full now, you will go hungry. How terrible for you who laugh now, you will mourn and weep. How terrible when all people speak well of you, their ancestors said the very same things about the false prophets."

Do you get the difference? There is a note of authority coming in now. There is not someone vaguely feeling after homespun proverbs. There is somebody saying: this is the better way. There is somebody speaking with absolute authority – happy are you who weep; sorrow is better than laughter; woe to you who laugh for you will weep.

There is a note of wisdom coming through, and Jesus taught that there were two sorts of people listening to him. There are those who are wise who will listen to what I say and go away and do it – and they are like a wise man who has built his house on the rock and when the crisis comes in the future that man's life will stand. Those who listened to his words and did nothing about them were fools building on sand, and when the crisis comes in the future, they would tumble down. This is where wisdom is beginning to be found. You will never read wiser words than Jesus taught.

You will never find wiser proverbs than on the lips of Jesus. He speaks with knowledge of life and an assurance. He took the longer perspective and he looked beyond the grave. Insults don't hurt you, they do the opposite. You should rejoice because great is your reward in heaven. Take the long-term view. The issue is not just what will I be like in old age, but what I will be like after I die if I pursue a certain course now. What is the ultimate outcome in eternity of what I do tomorrow? That is the long perspective and that is real wisdom. Real wisdom is not just considering my old age and providing for it. It is considering my life beyond old age and how I am preparing for it. This was the perspective that Jesus always took.

I still have not told you where wisdom is to be found, and I tell you now. It is to be found on a hill. You can only find wisdom on one hill in the entire world. "Men dig the mountains", says Job. They dig for gold, they dig for crystals, they dig for precious stones. Beneath the fields that grow our food they are smashing the mountain to pieces to try and find a vein of gold, to try and find something. But where shall wisdom be found? Look at 1 Corinthians 1:18–31.

Christ is the wisdom of God, and the message of the Cross is the power of God, to those who are being saved. For what seems to be God's foolishness is wiser than human wisdom and what seems to be God's weakness is stronger than human strength. That passage is where you find wisdom, and poor Ecclesiastes was groping after wisdom. He knew that this was the secret to life. I tell you, there is only one place in the world you will ever find real wisdom and that is at the foot of the cross on a hill called Calvary outside Jerusalem, and that is where life begins to make sense. That is where the real meaning begins to penetrate our darkened mind. That is where you see something that looks so silly, so foolish. This perfect life being thrown away on a cross at the age of thirty-three – that seems so mad, so crazy! Yet, as you look, you see that it is God's way of putting the world right. That is the place where you discover real life. That is the place where it makes sense. That is where the world's cleverness becomes foolishness and that is where God's "foolishness" is seen to be the wisest way.

Real wisdom is born. Job asked where it would be found. You dig for things, you search for things, but where do you find wisdom? You find wisdom when you go to the foot of the cross. You look at it and say: God, my mind can't grasp it. I don't understand it that your Son's death on that cross should be the means of putting the whole world right. I don't understand it but I know you are a very wise God.

How wise of God to make it this way. You see, if he had made it possible for men in their wisdom to find him, then philosophers would be the first into heaven. But this way I can get in. How wise! So God put his Son on a cross. The message is: come and look at that, and believe that he died for you, and you have taken the first step of wisdom. It will be the wisest step you ever took in your life and the step that is going to lead on to an understanding of the ultimate outcome of everything you do. That is the long perspective. You stand at the cross and you look into eternity and at last you say: "I understand."

Read Ecclesiastes 7:26–8:15

One of the things I had to do at Cambridge was to study philosophy. I got into a real turmoil doing that, and at points came very near to the brink of losing my own faith. When you listen to what people think, and the answers they try to give, it really does disturb. I am glad I didn't study philosophy at Oxford because in the standard philosophy examination there, one of the main questions was: how do you know that you are not dreaming? That is a philosophical question, and you can think it through. You have to give logical, reasonable answers as to why you are convinced that at this very moment you are not dreaming and that you are actually conscious and awake. It is a very difficult thing to prove, as most questions are when you get down to thinking about them, and indeed many schools of philosophy finish up in a kind of despair, a cynicism, a doubt about almost everything. There was one famous philosopher we were told about (Descartes) who came to one conclusion. There was only one thing he was sure about in life, and he expressed it in Latin: *cogito, ergo sum* [I think, therefore I am].

I have met philosophers who would not have been sure whether the pulpit in my church was there or not. They had thought so much they could not decide what was real and what was not. Of course, this is the reason why many people do not want to think at all. Indeed, if they stopped to think they would be so disturbed, so upset, that they would not be able to face life.

So we live in a world that is designed to help us not to

think. You see, if you don't want to think, you had better live a very busy life. You had better move very quickly through it, and you had better have as much noise as possible because in order to think you need quiet and you need to be still – you need time. So when you have the radio blaring the whole time, you are excused thinking.

You can drive through life at that speed; you can rush through this crazy world with all its noise, its clamour, its mass media telling you what to think so you can accept the views of the latest newscaster or the latest headline in the newspaper. You don't need to think because, if you stop to think, there is hardly anything at all that we can be sure of and that is disturbing. You cannot be sure of your job. You may be worried about it because you can't be sure of it if there is redundancy coming in your firm. You cannot be sure of your home. Are you going to be able to manage tax increases? You cannot be sure of your children. You cannot be sure of your government. You cannot be sure of your future, the way things are heading. You cannot be sure of your pension.

When you stop to think, and try to make a list of what you can be sure of in this world, it is a very short list. In fact, some would only have to write one word. The only thing I can be sure of is death – and that doesn't cheer you up very much. So let us not think, let us turn up the noise even louder and let us rush around, go here and go there. Let us be like one of these tourists who just has to see something new, who just has to be on the move to stop thinking. But the writer of Ecclesiastes was willing to sit down and think. We have explored with him what he thought about money, education, pleasure, wealth and wisdom. We have seen that every one of these explorations of discovery led to a dead end. Now we come to his exploration into human relationships – between men and women, between citizens and the king, between criminals and God. He is exploring all these relationships, trying to find the point, trying to find the meaning, trying to see some kind of purpose in life, and we will explore with him. I am afraid he is going to come up with the conclusion that he is not sure of anything except his lunch.

Let us first of all look at the social relationships he explores. The first main thing that I notice is that he is not sure of other people, particularly women, and we have to ask why. Now I realise I am treading on very thin ice here. I feel like the lecturer who had in his notes at the side: "Argument weak; shout here." But let us look very carefully at what he does say and what he doesn't, because I want to be absolutely fair to both the men and the women. Let me say, first of all, that the gap between his views on men and his views on women is very small. His views on women are only fractionally worse – to be precise 0.1% worse, so that is not a huge difference. Who could find wisdom? He found one man out of a thousand, but not one woman. Let us not get too excited about this. Having said that, I will return to what he thinks about men. I think that it is in itself a damning indictment that 99.9 percent of men cannot be respected. He was very near to our Lord's outlook here. Jesus would have said a hundred percent, but the writer of Ecclesiastes said 99.9 percent, so the latter had met someone somewhere whom at least he thought he could respect. But why did he not find one woman? Well I will tell you why, as far as I can see. There are seven reasons, and they explain to me why his different attitude was point one percent worse. The first thing is that it becomes quite clear from this passage that he had a very unfortunate first experience, and this coloured the thinking for the rest of his life – that is always a sad thing. But there is no doubt that your first serious relationship with someone of the opposite sex leaves its mark for the rest of your life, good or bad. Unfortunately for him the first one was a baddie, and he escaped. He tells us how he escaped from the relationship. He escaped by asking for God's help, and that is the only way a man will escape from that situation. He says it's a fate worse than death.

We usually talk about a woman in the clutches of a bad man as being in a fate worse than death, but he said that man in the clutches of a bad woman is a fate worse than death. His reply could be paraphrased: you won't get out with your own help, but you will with God's help. But he did not escape undamaged. That, I think, is the first reason, and it put up a barrier in him for all his later relationships.

Secondly, I believe that this man's position, his wealth, his education, all that he had, which he describes in the early chapters, attracted the wrong kind of woman into his life. So he became disillusioned.

A third reason is that he cast his net far too wide, and that comes out in this passage. He discovered this about women little by little. Now what does that tell you? He tried, and he tried, and he tried again. Therefore, there is a sad poignancy to his advice in chapter 9: Be content with the woman you married; stay with one; don't try to find as I did the perfect answer, one after the other, after the other.

You know it is almost pathetic when a public figure says: "You know, this time it is for keeps. The eighth time is really going to be it." You want to take them back to Ecclesiastes and say: you will discover what many have discovered, that you are expecting too much from your partner. Of course, this is the deepest reason why he came to this disillusionment. He was looking not for a person but for an answer. He calls women "answers", and an answer is not a person. He was looking for an answer to his own needs, an answer to his own question. He was not looking for a person to share life with, he was looking for an answer. He said that he did not find it, and he became disillusioned.

I think the final reason I would give you about why he came to this conclusion was simply that one of the first things sin spoiled was the relationship between man and woman, and this man was a sinner. Now if you add all those things together, notice he is not making a universal statement. He is not saying that you cannot trust any woman. What he is saying is: "I have found...." It is the sad testimony of someone who is really saying more about himself than about women here. It is an insight into his character that he has to say, sadly, "I have not found...." I could well believe that among all the women he met there was one who could have been just right for him, who could have answered his need had he been in a fit condition to spot her. But for the reasons I have stated he is saying quite sadly: I found none.

Of course, it was natural for him as a man to hope to find the answer in a woman. But you know, one of the great advantages of being a Christian in marriage is that you do not expect your spouse to meet your every need. You know that that is beyond any human being to do. Because you know Jesus Christ, who can meet the deep needs that even your own partner cannot meet, then you do not expect too much of each other, and you can treat each other as people.

That is the first disillusionment, but let us come back to the men, because the heart of this passage is what he has to say about both men and women. He is saying that you can hardly find anyone to respect. We have noticed that 0.1% difference between men and women, but the important thing he is affirming is that God made us all plain, simple people, and we have made ourselves complicated – and that is the heart of the problem.

How did he come to this conclusion? It is a far-reaching one and a beautiful statement to say: God made me plain and simple, but I have become complicated. That word "complicated" is similar to the word "complex". I think every

119

one of us has probably got some kind of a "complex" locked up in us which has complicated life for us. It has made life not a plain and simple thing, but a very complicated thing in which we have wrong reactions to people and situations. Who gave us our complexes? The answer, the writer realises, is that we gave them to ourselves. Like a snowball building up in life, we had a wrong reaction that began to roll and began to pick up other things with it. Gradually, what began as a very simple thing became a very complex thing, and someone might suffer now from a complex that destroys relationships, that prevents them serving the Lord freely, that enters into their dealings with other people in church. Thus life becomes so complicated. How did Ecclesiastes come to this conclusion – that man originally was a plain, simple creature, and that God was not responsible for our complexes? God didn't make us complicated. We made ourselves that way. It is not our fate to have complexes, it is our fault. How did he come to that conclusion?

Extraordinarily, he came to it by studying people's faces. He noticed that when we smile we have a plain and simple face and when we frown we have a very complicated one. What a profound observation. You know, when you are frowning you are using sixty-seven facial muscles. When you are smiling you are using sixteen, so life is a good deal simpler and less hard work. Why is it that some people have plain, simple, smiling faces and others have very complicated frowning faces? It is because when you have found the answer you smile and your face goes simple. But when you are still looking for it your face is all puckered up and complicated.

If you watch a television quiz show you will find that to be so. A question is asked of the team, their faces go all complicated but one person's face goes simple – have you noticed that? The buzzer is pressed and the face relaxes, a semi-smile comes, and the smile says: "I know. You're not going to catch me up with that one." There is a simple reaction. The writer, studying people's faces, noticed how complicated many faces get and how frowning they become. How simple a face becomes when you have found the answer.

So he came to the conclusion that there were so many complexes around and so complicated was life because people had not found the answer. I know that when he looked into the mirror he saw a very complicated face. He was a man who had not found an answer and so he was complicating himself.

His thoughts here could be paraphrased: God made us plain and simple, and so he made us to know the answers to life, and we don't know the answers, and when we fail to find them we become complicated people, and life gets hard and tough. The New Testament has a lovely phrase about the simplicity that is "in Christ". A person who really finds the answers in Jesus Christ becomes a simple person. I don't mean naïve, I just mean straightforward.

In saying he is not sure of people the writer is really saying he is not sure of himself. In fact, a man who makes that kind of remark about women is unsure of himself. It is not that he is not sure of women.

Now the second thing: he is not sure of the authorities. I can understand this kind of feeling. I have to confess that I made it my business at school to keep out of the way of the headmaster. When I joined the Forces, even though I went in as an officer, that did not give me self-confidence with the senior officers and I kept out of their way. I will never forget my ghastly first parade when I saluted a man three ranks below me because I didn't recognise his badge, and was written off as a greenhorn straightaway. But we had the senior officer right there in our station, and I just kept out of the way of the Air Commodore. If I got into his way then I did what I was told and got out of his way as quickly as possible. Some have the same attitude to their boss – don't get into trouble, do what you're told, just keep out of the way of those in authority. The writer of Ecclesiastes came to identical conclusions when he thought about someone's relationship to the king. The person could never be quite sure of the mood the king would be in. So he was unsure of himself in this setting with somebody who had greater power than he had and had greater authority and he was a little insecure. So his advice could be summarised: Do what the king tells you but don't stay in his presence; it is a dangerous place to be.

Up at college in Cambridge there was a high table and then a number of low tables. At the high table the tutors and the Principal sat, but there was also room for about half a dozen students at that high table, and it was always the last to be filled. I noticed that we all grabbed the low tables, and then the few that could not get a place on the low tables found themselves at the high table, poor things. I am afraid I developed a very neat art of getting one of the chairs at the low tables. So his message is: I'm unsure of the authorities; I'm unsure of the king; I'm unsure so I don't quite know when is the right time to go to him with a petition – I don't know if he's in a good mood today; life is really terribly insecure with the persons who are over you. You are never quite sure where you are with them, so do what they tell you but keep out of their way as much as you can. It is sound advice but it doesn't get you very far.

Here is a man filled with insecurity. The next thing he is not sure of is the future. No one can tell him what is going to happen next week, and this gives him a feeling of being unsure. This is very common. Why is it that so many thousands of our fellow countrymen read their horoscope?

They look straight up to see what their star is and what is going happen to them. They are so insecure they want to know what is going to happen even during the next twenty-four hours, and if they are going to come into a fortune and meet an attractive stranger. Somehow this gives them a little feeling that life is slightly more sure.

The writer of Ecclesiastes says that the one thing he is not sure about is his life, his future. The one thing that he can be certain of is that he cannot cheat death – it is going to come. He is going to be in a coffin one day. So that makes him unsure. Then he moves on. He is writing a list all the time, of the things he cannot be sure of.

The next thing he cannot be sure of, and one of the biggest and most disturbing is justice. That is an awful insecurity. He gives us three reasons why he can't. Number one: because power is unevenly distributed. He notices that there are some people in this world who have the power and there are others who have to suffer under them, and that makes him insecure. The second reason is that public opinion is so fickle that if you rely on it you will find that overnight it can switch to the very opposite of what it was. Therefore, public justice can fail. He cites the case of a wicked man who is buried, and on the way back from his funeral everybody is saying what a wonderful man he is.

The third reason you cannot trust justice is that crime is not punished quickly enough. But it was horrifying when, (in a foreign country) a man was caught stealing some fruit or something from a stall in the marketplace. Within half an hour he had been caught and punished publicly in the middle of the marketplace.

Ecclesiastes teaches that if crime were dealt with as soon as it took place, it would stop. That is a profound observation because the writer applies it not only to human retribution but wants to know why God does not deal with sin as soon as it arises. Why doesn't he make this a moral world in which as soon as a man has sinned he is punished? Here the writer fights against what he had been taught, namely that if you obey God and do what is right you will be rewarded whereas if you disobey God you will die young. It is a simple equation that many people assume: that if you are good it pays and if you are bad, you will be punished, therefore, it pays to be good; honesty is the best policy. Ecclesiastes indicates that if you look at life you will see that it is immoral. You will see that the righteous often get the punishment due to the wicked, and the wicked often get the reward due to the righteous. God, why don't you punish immediately? Why don't you put it right immediately? It would stop sin if you punished it as soon as a person did it.

Why then does God let this go on, even right to death, so that nobody can see his moral principles working out in this life? I am afraid that is one of the biggest questions you ask when you are honest about life. Why does God wait before punishing sin? Why does he wait so long that people's consciences are deadened and they forget about the sins they have committed? Why does he not teach them a lesson now so that they might learn? It is a big question.

But the writer is not even sure that God rewards goodness and punishes badness because he doesn't see him doing it. So, having made his list, he is not sure of people, particularly in his case women; he is not sure of himself. He has made himself so complicated. He is not sure of his own future. He is not sure of human justice and not even sure of divine justice. What then can he be sure of? There is only one thing and he says that the only things he can be sure of are the simple pleasures that he can enjoy by himself. I find this sad.

Once again we realise so clearly that if your limits to human wisdom are what you can discover under the sun and before you die, then that is the philosophy you are left with. It is the philosophy of probably three-quarters of our fellow countrymen today who will have a good Sunday lunch and go to the pub for a drink and come home and watch television, and that is the purpose of life. That is the point of life, and that is as far as they can get, and it is the one thing they are sure of. They are not sure of their job, their home, their pension, their future or anything else. You can see what a self-centred philosophy it is: having said you cannot respect or trust others, Ecclesiastes has to say the only thing is to enjoy yourself.

That is why it is understandable that so many of our fellow countrymen live as they live. It is the logical conclusion. They have come to it instinctively and immediately, whereas, Ecclesiastes went half way around the world to find it out. He explored it with his mind. He thought about it; he tried it. He explored as far as he could and he came back to where most people are anyway and said: that is all you can do.

I find it extremely poignant that men and women who were made in the image of God, who were made with eternity in their minds, as Ecclesiastes says, who were made for God, who were made for something much bigger than this world, who were made to rise above the sun, who were made for heaven itself, have come to the conclusion that the best thing you can do is have a Sunday lunch and a pint at the pub and watch television – but you can understand it.

I finish by telling you the good news. If there is no security finally in loving women, if there is no security finally in obeying authority, if there is no security finally in even doing what you believe God wants you to do in this world, I tell you there is security in Jesus Christ. When I turn to the teaching of Jesus I find that he said many of the things that Ecclesiastes said; his observation on life was just as keen – indeed perfectly accurate. But he came to totally different conclusions. It is fascinating that Jesus had an even lower respect for human beings than Ecclesiastes because he spoke of 100% of people, he didn't say 99.9%.

One of the most startling statements made of Jesus is made in John's Gospel at the end of chapter 2 where it says: many put their trust in Jesus but he would not put his trust in any of them because he knew what was in man. What a statement! Yet he did not despair. He was so sure of himself that he was able to give himself to those who trusted him – even though he knew them through and through, even though he was under no illusions about human nature, even though he knew about the complexes, even though he knew how complicated they had made their lives.

Mary Magdalene could come to him with such a complicated life. She was mixed up with men, with demons. Jesus didn't say, "This is a wonderful woman underneath." No, Jesus knew that he was a wonderful Saviour. He trusted his own power to straighten out that woman's life. So she became a simple woman, she lost her complex. She loved Jesus, and his love for her created in her the simplicity that was the secret of life, and this madwoman became one of the loveliest women you can imagine.

Zacchaeus was a man who got all his accounts very complicated. My, how he fiddled them only he knew. His relationships were all complicated and he was a man of such complexes that people would not let him through to the front of the crowd. He was a little man so he climbed up a tree and he got up that tree, and Jesus said, "Zacchaeus, come down." Jesus was going to get that man's life straightened out that day and get him back to being a plain, simple person. Zacchaeus's attitude we could paraphrase as: If I've been wronging people I'll get them repaid. I want to get things straight and simple, get my books simple.

Jesus was just going through life. He didn't trust any man because he knew what was in man. But he trusted in himself because he trusted in his Father and that made his life very simple. Because when you look at the life of Jesus you see, essentially, a very simple life, a life untrammelled and uncomplicated. It was a life, for example, that had perfect relationships with women, because he was not looking for an answer in them. He was looking for people. He was not trying to meet his own need; he was trying to meet theirs. You find, therefore, that in every situation he met it so simply with utter confidence. You couldn't find in Jesus any trace of a complex. You try. Get the best psychiatrist you know to go through the life of Jesus and find a complex. No, his life was simple.

If the wind and the waves were threatening his disciples he just stood up and said: "Peace, be still." How simple. In a situation where the disciples were tearing their hair because they couldn't help someone, Jesus said, "Oh, how long am I going to be with you? Bring him to me." Quite simply, he dealt with it. Here was a person who was sure of God his Father and who could say before he did a miracle: Thank you Father that you heard me. Here was someone who had this absolute trust in the Father so that he could relate to men and women and he could relate to those in authority. He knew the wisdom of getting out of the authority's way. That is why he was often crossing the Sea of Galilee in a boat. If you study a map you find that even though the Sea of Galilee is a tiny lake there were three different territories sharing its shores. When Jesus got into a boat to cross the lake, it was simply to get out of the way of an authority, Herod or someone else. He knew the wisdom of when to put himself in the hands of the authorities and when to keep out of their hands, and yet there came a day when he chose to die. To me this is perhaps the most wonderfully simple thing about Jesus: that he knew when it was right to die. He decided when it would be, where it would be, how it would be.

You don't need to pity Jesus as he goes to the cross, for he had chosen this. He is not the victim, he is the victor. He is not being trapped by circumstances, he is in charge of those circumstances. No man takes his life from him. He lays it down of his own free will – what a simplicity there is. It is when people come to know Jesus Christ, which is something the writer of Ecclesiastes was not in a position to do, alas, but we who live in anno domini can come to know Jesus Christ – the things that happen then are that we gain the confidence, the assurance, to relate to people. We then gain the confidence to face our death. We then gain certain assurances which make us people not with a long list of things we are not sure about, but with a long list of things we are sure about.

At last, when I listen to Jesus I understand why God does not punish sin immediately, why life seems to be so immoral. He taught us that it is very simple, really. You see, God is letting the wheat and the tares grow up together. He is not pulling the tares out as soon as they appear. Because if he did pull the tares out there would be nothing left to grow, you would pull the young wheat out also. So he is letting both grow together, but one day he will separate them, and the wheat will be gathered into his barn and the tares will be burned. What a simple answer to the question. If God rooted out of our society every person who sinned as soon as they sinned, just ask yourself: would anything be left? Would anyone be left to grow and be harvested? The answer is: not one person; and God intends to have a harvest. So he lets good and evil go on growing together. He lets evil people get away with it. But let them be absolutely sure of this, for Jesus was absolutely sure and it comes out in parable after parable: "Whatever a man sows that shall he also reap." Story after story which Jesus told said that: the wheat and the tares grow together; the wise and the foolish virgins wait together; the good and the bad fish are caught in the net together. Yes, it is all mixed up together, but one day there will be a separation of wheat and tares, of good and bad fish, of wise and foolish virgins. One day the wrongs will be put right. One day God will act, and how wise he is to be patient with us.

We should see the apparent injustice of our world as a glorious token of God's patience with us in letting good and evil grow together, that some of us might be gathered into his barn. What mercy; what patience. So in Jesus Christ I become sure of judgment, I become sure that this is a moral universe. I become sure that things will be put right, and right will be rewarded and wrongs will be punished, because Jesus said that he is going to put it right. All the nations will be gathered together before him, the Son of Man.

In Jesus Christ I become sure of my future. I hear a voice say "I am the way", and I become sure. There are many things that a Christian is not sure about, and we need to admit them honestly and freely. There are questions that some people ask me that I cannot answer. I do not always know what, why or how something is the case. But the one thing I do know is *who*, and that brings me the assurance I need: "I know whom I have believed".

Ecclesiastes was not sure of anything except when he was enjoying himself. But when you are sure of Jesus, you are sure of everything worth having. You are sure that judgment is coming. You are sure that your sins can be forgiven. You are sure that heaven is being prepared for you. You are sure of Jesus – not sure of yourself, but sure of him. So we are thankful that Ecclesiastes reminds us how little we can be sure of in this world. But thank you Jesus for making us so sure of the next world that we can say with Paul, "I am persuaded that neither death, nor life, nor angels, nor principalities, nor powers, nor things present, nor things to come, nor height, nor depth, nor any other creature shall be able to separate us from the love of God which is in Christ Jesus." If you are sure of that, you can sit lightly to other things. If you are sure of that, you will not expect too much of your wife or husband – you will be able to treat them as a person. If you are sure of this, you will not be afraid of any authorities because, as with Jesus in front of Pontius Pilate, you can say to the highest authority in the land: "You would have no power over me unless it were given you from above."

If you are sure of Jesus, you are sure that crime does not pay and sin does not pay, and that the accounts will be settled. So with Jesus comes the security we need to live simple lives – uncomplicated; without complexes. Plain and simple folk we may be, but thank God for making us that.

Read Ecclesiastes 8:16-9:12

Quite frankly, if we didn't know Jesus Christ we would have to agree with every word of that passage. Praise God we don't have to agree because we know Jesus. In chapter 7 we read that it is better to attend funerals than festivals, because the living should always remind themselves that death is waiting for us all. We are reminded in this passage now that no one knows when that day will come and it can happen quite unexpectedly.

It is good for us to have reminders, to be brought up short, to be reminded that nobody is here forever, and no family circle is secure, and that death is the greatest fact of life.

Therefore I have encapsulated the passage in a single question: if we are going to die tomorrow, what shall we do today? The answer is: that depends on what happens the day after tomorrow.

To put it in a very different way, what we believe about life after death decides how we behave during life before death. It is what we believe concerning beyond the grave that is going to decide what we do with our time this side of it. This passage highlights the fact that the Old Testament says hardly anything about life after death. Had that ever struck you? You try to think of clear teaching in the Old Testament about what lies beyond the grave, and you are up against a real problem. It is not that they didn't believe in life after death in that age, they did.

I was fascinated to study the excavations of Tutankhamun's

tomb when some of the treasures found within it were brought to London, and to see how they really believed that Tutankhamun would need furniture, chariots, clothes and gold, and would in fact need the body beyond the grave, so they preserved it as best they knew how. They really believed that there was a life beyond, and that he would need all those goods for it, so they put those things in that tomb. What to me was so pathetic was that when they opened the tomb they were all there, covered in dust, unused.

Now it is against that background that the Old Testament was written. In Egypt and in Babylon, people believed very clearly in life after death. They buried things in the grave for people to use the other side of death. But the Israelites did not talk like that – they were different. They were, I believe, more honest. They faced the facts and so they used all the euphemisms which we use. We don't like to say "so and so died." We say: "They have fallen asleep," and the Hebrews used that euphemism. They said, "He died and slept with his fathers." They didn't give any indication as to whether he was going to wake up from that sleep, whether he was conscious, semi-conscious or unconscious. It is just a blank.

In fact, the more they thought about it, the more they came to the conclusion that the dead were not conscious and not active, and if their spirits survived the separation from their bodies then their spirits floated on in some vague existence, to which they gave the term Sheol – that is the Hebrew word; in Greek, "Hades", the world of the dead. I have heard it best described by an Old Testament scholar in Cambridge as a kind of station waiting room with no trains coming, where spirits just wait, doing nothing, saying nothing, thinking nothing, and in the Psalms it comes out. We read Psalm 30, "Will it help you, God, if I go down to the world of the dead. Do the dead praise you? Can the dead give you anything? Then you've saved me, and I can praise you. And I praise you for it, that you didn't let me go down to the world of the dead where nothing can happen."

Ecclesiastes has this very sombre view of death. Its writer says: "They don't have any love, they don't have any hate, they don't have any passion. All these things died with them. Work hard at whatever you do because there will be no action, no thought, no knowledge, no wisdom in the world of the dead." Ecclesiastes is going strictly on scientific observation. As far as we can see, to die is to cease to exist. As far as we can see, it is oblivion. As far as we can see, that is the end of a person. They are out of the scene of activity. They are off the stage and they will soon be forgotten. Now, that is being utterly honest. I believe the Hebrews were more honest than the Egyptians.

The Hebrews faced facts and they said: as far as we can see, it is better to face the fact that we have got to find God in this life; we have got to enjoy God in this life – because once you get to the end of it you get to the end of praise and of prayer, you get to the end of thought, of action, of wisdom, your little light goes out. This is why they desperately tried to work out God's providence within this life. They desperately tried to say that if God is a moral God then it is this life where reward and punishment must take place, because everybody finishes in the grave the same way. Therefore, if God is a moral God, if this is a moral universe, then the righteous have to be rewarded here and now, and the evil have to be punished here and now. But when they looked at the here and now, that did not seem to happen. This is the great dilemma, the great enigma of life, which Ecclesiastes highlights.

Starting from this premise that death is the end and there is no conscious life for the individual beyond it, the writer tries to work out what God does here and to see the pattern of his providence here – what he rewards here and punishes here. He came to the conclusion that nobody can answer that question; that even if you stayed awake all night and thought and thought and teased this subject around in your mind and asked on what principles God operates within this life, you would have to come to the conclusion: "I don't know."

The worst thing he says here, unfortunately, does not always come out too clearly in translation. It is that if there is nothing beyond death and you ask what kind of a God you can see active and operating in this life, he had to say that he does not even know whether God loves him or hates him, meaning: I cannot tell from my experience of life whether the power up there who created me likes me or dislikes me; I cannot tell if he wants to do me good or do me harm; I cannot tell whether he is well disposed or ill-disposed towards me. So he was left with this horrible, empty view of life.

If you do not believe in life after death, this is the only conclusion you can come to – that we do not know whether God loves us or hates us. We do not know if the things that we think should matter to God really do, because he seems indifferent to them. If God really is good then he would see that the innocent do not suffer; he would see that the wicked do. He would see that a good deed is rewarded; he would see that an evil deed is not rewarded but punished. He would see that honesty and chastity paid, and he would see that dishonesty and unchastity did not pay. He would see to that, but he doesn't.

In this life we are left with this question: does God love us or hate us? It is a depressing picture, but a very realistic one. We must face it honestly before we move on to the good news of Jesus Christ. The writer goes as far as to say that the poorest living creature is better than the finest dead one. A dog was the most despised animal in the Middle East. They did not keep them as pets, they were wild scavengers, and yet he said that "a living dog is better than a dead lion" – the finest creature of the jungle, the king of the beasts. But once a lion is dead, then a living dog is better off. The living at least know they are going to die, but the dead know nothing.

These are huge statements. They have been echoed in the human heart ever since. A man called Lessing went to visit Egypt and stood in front of the Sphinx – that great creature they dug out of the sand with that very strange Mona Lisa expression, and you are supposed to be able to go and ask it questions. Lessing said when he stood in front of the Sphinx that he wanted to ask only one question of it, namely: is this a friendly universe?

Dick Shepherd, from St. Martin in the Fields, said he once stood on a dark, starlit night all alone and he wanted to shout up into the darkness: "Friend or foe?" Am I in the hands of a God who is favourable to me or antagonistic?

When life has battered you about a bit you sometimes wonder about that question, and you sometimes ask it from the depths of your heart: Does God love me or hate me? Is he really trying to help me to be good? Because it doesn't seem to be paying right now. That is an honest question.

So the writer of Ecclesiastes is asking what the point is of being religious. What is the point of being good? We all finish up the same place. Or, as a grave digger said to a visitor looking around a churchyard, "I get them all in the end." The visitor wanted to reply, "Ah, but it will get you too in the end." Is that all that has to be said? What then can we do with life if that is all?

Ecclesiastes is nothing if not positive, and the Jews managed to live for centuries without a clear view of life after death. How did they do it? They did it by affirming life. They did it with that toast "L'chaim" which means: "To life!" If you have seen *Fiddler on the Roof* you have seen a marvellous picture of Jewish life: weighed down with the suffering that could come tomorrow it nevertheless affirmed life while it could, drank to life, enjoyed life, made the most of every passing opportunity to enjoy what God had given. This was the practical philosophy, and it is the best one for those who don't believe in life after death. If you believe that death is oblivion, if you believe that when someone dies that is the last you will see of them and that is the last time you will speak to them – if you believe that, then the very best thing you can do is to seize every opportunity you can to enjoy life, to enjoy every blessing, because you won't have it too long, so enjoy it now. It may be appropriate to read: Go ahead eat your food and be happy, drink your wine and be cheerful; it is alright with God. The Hebrews believed it was alright with God. I want to say it is alright with God. He has given us all things freely for us to enjoy and it is right to enjoy them. God did not want us to be in a lovely, beautiful world that he made and be miserable. He wanted us to seize life; he wanted us to have these things. So go ahead, be cheerful, enjoy yourself, cheer yourself up, cheer other people up. Do it, because tomorrow you are going to die. Work hard because you are more likely to be cheerful if you are working hard than if you have nothing to do. That is certainly true.

But if that were all that God had to say to us, do you think we could go on enjoying life? If God had remained hidden from us, and if God had so hidden his providential principles that no one could say what he is on about, and what he is trying to do with us, and what he made the world for – if all we could say was, "Well, let's enjoy ourselves because we're quite sure that God wanted us to do that" – is that enough?

I remember reading a sermon illustration used by a preacher who said: "I want you to imagine that a lot of people went on a cruise in the Pacific Ocean. They got on board a luxury liner. They had everything they could ask for; they had the most gorgeous food, they danced every night, they had a party every night, they swam all day, they sunbathed.

They had so much, they had all this, and they were enjoying themselves thoroughly until the captain said: "Ladies and gentlemen, I've got great news for you: this ship is going nowhere. You can go on enjoying every day as long as you like. We are just going to circle the Pacific Ocean so that you can go on enjoying yourself." From that day people began to be miserable. From that day they began to lose the enjoyment of the cruise. From that day you could see people sitting around the deck with long faces."

You see, you cannot ultimately enjoy even the good things God has given you unless there is some sense of purpose, unless you have some idea as to what God is doing and what he is after and what his providence is preparing you for, and whether you are going somewhere or not. There is within us this tension: Alright, let's enjoy ourselves, because death is oblivion. Somehow we cannot live with that thought. Somehow we have got to press through. Somehow we have got to try to find some further truth about life after death, but Ecclesiastes has not got it and the writer never got through.

But when Jesus Christ came he altered the whole scene. By the time Jesus was born there were two sorts of Jew. They had already divided into at least two denominations. This happens to all religions. The two denominations were Pharisees and Sadducees, and the big argument between them was whether there was life after death. From exile there came back Jews who said that there must be life after death, and they became known as the Pharisees. It was into that situation that Jesus came. The other group was the Sadducee party who did not believe in life after death. Great arguments went on between these two groups and they tried to see which side Jesus was going to be on in this matter. The Sadducees came to him one day and told him about someone who had lost their spouse seven times, and asked who were they going to be married to if there was to be a resurrection, and wasn't

137

there going to be an awful mix-up in heaven when they all got together again? They were laughing at the idea of life after death. Jesus came out very clearly on the Pharisees' side of the argument. He told them that if they searched scripture carefully they would get their answer.

In fact, when you search the Old Testament very carefully indeed, you find tiny glimpses of a life after death – they are there. There is the confidence that Job had: "Yet in my flesh I will see God" – a leap of faith, but it was there. You find it also in the psalmist when he was wrestling with the problem of the innocent suffering and the wicked escaping. Then he recognised what their end was, and he wrote: "That you will guide me with your counsel and *afterward* you'll receive me into glory."

You can find maybe a couple of dozen glimpses, no more, through the Old Testament: little chinks of light, as if a door was slightly ajar and you could see through it into something beautiful and glorious just beyond. But when Jesus came he flung the door wide open. Let us say, first, that Jesus taught unmistakably that the dead survive with conscious life and memory. Can you realise what a shock that was to the Jews? But Jesus taught absolutely clearly that five minutes after you are dead, you will be conscious – you will know that you have survived. He left us in no doubt whatever about that. In his parables he mentions it, but above all Jesus spoke of the God of Abraham and Isaac and Jacob. Why does he say: "I am the God of Abraham and Isaac and Jacob" instead of saying: I *was* the God of Abraham and Isaac and Jacob? Because Abraham, Isaac and Jacob are still around, and he is still their God.

On the top of the Mount of Transfiguration Jesus spoke with Moses and Elijah, and they had been dead and gone for centuries. But he chatted with them about his cross and his death and the exodus he was going to accomplish in

138

Jerusalem. So, again and again, Jesus made it quite clear that people who have died are conscious and can talk and can have relationships. Above all, there is the glorious truth that he raised the dead. So when they came to the grave of Lazarus, he spoke to a dead body and said: "Lazarus, come out of there," and Lazarus came out. He also did it with the widow of Nain's son and Jairus's daughter.

It is interesting that it was the Sadducees who put Jesus in the grave. It was the Sadducees that sealed the tomb. Their understanding would have been: that's it, there is no life after death; we are finished with him; he is in that tomb, he is dead, and he has gone and we have dealt with him and we will never hear any more of him – it is over; it has finished. The Sadducees did not believe in life after death, but three days later that stone was rolled away and Jesus was back again.

Furthermore, he has revealed to us in his Word the most astonishing thing. During the three days his body lay in that grave, do know what Jesus was doing? Do you think he was asleep and unconscious? He was preaching, and he was preaching to the people who had been drowned in Noah's flood. It is one of the most extraordinary little touches in the New Testament, that between his death and resurrection Jesus was preaching to people who had been dead for centuries, drowned in the days of Noah.

So we get this tremendous sense that someone who is dead is conscious, active, relating. It is like a breakthrough in thinking about life after death. For the first time it is based not on speculation, not on embalming bodies or putting furniture into graves, it is based on an empty tomb and someone who came back and who was the same person. Survival after death is the first clear thing that we must get into our minds when we listen to Jesus. His words and his works make it absolutely clear that death is not the end of conscious life.

The second thing that Jesus made clear is this: that life

beyond death is a life that has been unmixed. Now let me tell you what I mean. In this world we have a mixture of light and darkness, we have a mixture of life and death, we have a mixture of disease and health, we have a mixture of ugliness and beauty. One thing is absolutely clear in Jesus' teaching about life after death: life is unmixed. There are two kinds of life after death and only two, and light is on one side and darkness is on the other. Health is on one side and disease is on the other. Beauty is on one side, and ugliness is on the other. Life is on one side, and death is on the other. He made it quite clear that life after death was not going to be in a mixed world any more. At last there would be a good world and an evil world, and not a mixture. That will answer a lot of questions.

In fact, there won't be the questions raised in that situation. At last there will be a world in which God can be clearly seen as a good God, as God who is light, God who is love. It will be a world in which there will be no hate, no pride, no envy, no anger, no lust – none of the things that spoil this world, and that spoil the very best of us, but a world in which these things have been separated, and between them is a great gulf so that they can never get mixed up again. That is the second thing that I get very clearly from Jesus Christ.

The third thing I get is that this is the pattern on which God in his providential care is working – that he is not going to separate these things in this world. He is going to separate them in the next. It is in the next life that wrongs will be put right. It is in the next life that evil will be punished and good rewarded. It is beyond the grave that God will do these things. You may say to me, "Well, why has God chosen to do it there and not here? Why does God leave us in a mixed situation? Why does he not sort it out here?" The answer is so obvious if you just think. If good were rewarded in this life, and if evil were immediately punished in this life, do you know you wouldn't be able to get into a church building for the queues? God would force us to be good, would he not? There would be no choice. If as soon as you did wrong you were filled with disease and as soon as you did right you got perfect health, would you not do right immediately? Of course you would – you would be forced to. There would be no choice about it; no faith needed, no trust, no freedom. But because we are in a mixed-up world in which it does not pay to be good you can choose to be good.

Somebody has said, "Honesty may be the best policy, but if it is the best policy it is not honesty." You live in a world in which you can choose to be honest, because if it always paid you would not choose. Do you follow me? This is a mixed up world in which good does not always pay and evil can pay off. Indeed, in this country crime does pay now because over sixty percent of the crimes in this country are not now detected, so it pays you to be a burglar now. You stand a better chance of getting away with it now. In that situation you can choose to be honest. You can choose not to steal because that is good and right. You can choose that right way by faith, believing that it will be rewarded but not here.

This will save you from the disillusionment that comes to many who say, "I've been so good, and look what is happened to me. I've tried to live a decent life." I think the most amusing situation that ever occurred to me was when I went hospital visiting and I met a man who was in his mid-nineties. He realised I was a minister and he said, "I've got a problem about God."

I said, "What's the problem?"

He replied, "Well, I just cannot believe in a good God." "Why not?"

"Well," he said, "what am I doing here in a hospital? I've lived a decent life. I've kept myself, and looked after myself, and I've looked after other people."

I said, "Just a moment, have you never been in hospital before?"

"Never."

I said, "Have you never been ill before?"

"Never. Why is God letting this happen to me?"

Ten days later he was out of that hospital and on his feet. He had just got his ideas all mixed up.

God has not made this world a world in which goodness pays. He has made this a world in which you may freely choose to be good. He has said, "Great is your reward in heaven..." – and that will see if you are really good, won't it? That will show if you trust that there is a good God. That gives you the opportunity to have faith that God will put wrongs right.

So that is the third thing that Jesus made quite clear. First, the survival of the individual in conscious relationship and activity. Second: two worlds, one of which is beautiful beyond description, marvellous beyond imagination, light, love, everything is in that world; and another world, which is dark, horrible and hateful. Now comes the big question: which world do you get into? Well, the answer is very simple. If you are good you will get into the good one and if you are bad you will get into the bad one. Does that settle it? Not quite. I wish it were that simple.

We had some intriguing interviews with boy entrants when they joined the Royal Air Force. As chaplain I had to meet them, and I remember I used to say, "How many Methodists here? How many Baptists? How many Brethren? How many agnostics? How many atheists? How many Christians?" Consternation! They would look at each other and no hands would go up. I would say, "Come on, how many Christians are there here?" Occasionally a hand would go straight up. They did not mind saying they were Methodists, Baptists or anything else. But when one said "How many Christians?"

there was real consternation.

So I said, "Come on, how many Christians?"

"Well, what do you mean, Padre?"

I said, "Well, what do *you* mean?"

They would say, "Well, somebody who keeps the Ten Commandments. That was always the first answer.

"Okay, that's fine, somebody who keeps the Ten Commandments. How many Christians are there here?"

Consternation again, hands going up and down. "Well, nobody can keep them all, Padre."

"Okay, how many do you have to keep?"

"Six out of ten" – that was invariably the proportion, their pass mark.

"Fine," I said, "six out of ten – how many Christians are there here?" Still hesitation.

How good do you have to be to get into that good world, Jesus?

Jesus says, "Well, you don't have to be good enough to be good in your own judgment nor good enough to be good in other people's judgment. There is only one thing: you need to be good enough in God's sight – that's all." That closes the kingdom of heaven to me so tightly. I reckon I could be good enough in my own sight, provided I was fairly tolerant with myself and lenient, and excuse certain things. I reckon I might just get away with it and be good enough in some other people's sight; not those who know me well, but some people I might get away with. But to be good enough in God's sight? Consider what his pass mark is. It is ten out of ten. Do you realise that if God allowed you into heaven as you are it would certainly spoil it for everybody else? Let that sink in. There is enough anger, pride or envy in you to spoil heaven. Jesus said that place is going to be good. It is going to be really good, really clean, really lovely. If you are really good, clean and lovely you can go there. But you are

143

not going there if you are going to spoil it. I am afraid the sad truth is that if any of us went as we are we would spoil it. Would you not agree? It would be hell for some people to live with me forever as I am – it would not be heaven. So we are left with this terrible impasse. I thought it was good news that Jesus brought. I thought he was going to bring life and immortality to light. I thought he was going to tell us that there was a wonderful life awaiting all of us beyond the grave. Now he has told us that the conditions for that good life are such that none of us stand a chance of getting there. So what do we do now?

Let us go back to Ecclesiastes. He posed questions: Is it love or is it hate? Friend or foe? Is this a friendly universe? Is God favourably disposed towards me or not? That is the question. The answer comes from the lips of Jesus: that "... whoever believes in him should not perish but have everlasting life". That word "perish" came home to me so forcibly when I realised that it meant exactly what it said. If you have had a hot water bottle perish you know what has happened to it. It has not ceased to exist. It has simply ceased to be able to be used for the purpose for which it was made. It is still there, but it is useless. A man who has perished has not gone into oblivion, he has just become useless for the purpose for which God made him. When God made man he made us to bear his image and reflect glory and be his sons and love him and love one another. When someone perishes that is when he has reached the point where he can no longer contain love, where he can no longer be the kind of person that God wanted him to be. Jesus, who was the only one in the Bible who really talked about hell, spoke of it in terms of such horror that he said that it would be better for you to pull your eyes out or cut your hand off than go to that place. It is a place where people have become useless for love. It is a place where they have perished as human beings. It is a place where they have just gone rotten and where they stink. God wanted nobody to land up in that place. How on earth then could he take me as I am and put me in a world where my sin would spoil it? Well, there is only one way and that was he had to deal with that sin. He had to get it out of my life. How could he do that? He did it first by sending Jesus to a cross. If Ecclesiastes couldn't see God's plan in this world, the day that Jesus died was surely the supreme example of this great conundrum: why do the innocent suffer and the guilty go scot-free? You may look at that scene and ask where God is in this; what does he think he is doing? Here is the only perfect life that has ever been lived, one life that deserved to be rewarded, and what does it get? A cross.

There is no sense, no rhyme, no reason in this and Ecclesiastes' perplexity comes to a peak at Calvary. You say, "God, what do you think you are doing? This is a mad world, it's not a moral world if that kind of thing can happen in it." But God knew what he was doing. God let it happen so that an innocent person might suffer on behalf of the guilty. Ever since then we have known that we need not question God's providence. We need not say, "Why did you let this happen?" God knows what he is doing.

That day when injustice was at its worst and when an innocent, perfect life was being cruelly, painfully done to death, God was achieving what he wanted. He was making it possible for David Pawson to go and live in a lovely world beyond the grave. He was making it possible for my sins to get forgiven. He was making it possible then by raising Jesus from the dead and giving him back to me, making it possible for me to be fit enough to go, and to begin a work in my heart that will go on until it is complete and until he has got me fit – that is what it was all about.

So I know what God is doing. The writer of Ecclesiastes, lying on his bed, awake day and night, was teasing his mind.

145

"Lord, what are you doing in this world? I can't see what you're doing." I know what God is doing. He is bringing many sons to glory, preparing people for another world. He is making people fit to live with him in glory. He is letting us go through the mill, letting us face suffering; he is letting us face the good and the bad, because "... we know that for those who love God all things work together for good, for those who are called according to his purpose."

It is his school, and school can be tough, but I know what he is doing. He has revealed it. So I now know the answer. Is it love or hate? The answer is: it is love. Lord, do you know what you are doing in this mess that we call planet earth? God does know what he is doing. He is preparing you for somewhere else that is far beyond anything you have ever seen or heard or imagined. It is a new world.

Ecclesiastes might appear to suggest that if there is nothing after death, the best thing you can do is enjoy yourself – eat your food, drink your wine. But the Christian says there is something more. This week will bring me one week nearer to heaven, and therefore should bring me one week nearer to being fit to go there. So it is not just, "Enjoy yourself now."

If we are going to die tomorrow, what shall we do today? That depends on the day after tomorrow. If the day after tomorrow is heaven then today must be the preparation for it. It can still affirm life. It can still enjoy all that God gives. It can still say, "L'chaim." But instead of just saying "To life" it says, "To eternal life!"

Read Ecclesiastes 9:13–11:6 and 12:9

I have found Ecclesiastes one of the saddest books in the Bible. Parts of it make very depressing reading. The tragedy is that it is written by a man who found out at the end of his life where he ought to have begun it. Do you not think that is a tragedy? For we only get one life to live and we only have one chance to live it. By the time he discovered the starting point of real life it was too late for him to begin the journey. But it was not too late for other people, and praise God he wrote it down for others so that they may not come as far as he had done before they would find out where you begin to live real life. He tried very hard to write a book that would comfort us and lift our spirits, but instead what came from him were real words that faced life as it really is. They are not comforting words but they are honest words.

At this point we will consider an overview of the whole book to try to help you to see the pattern of it and where it leads to, and then we will look at the very last section of it.

The writer was trying to find out what is life all about. How do you discover its meaning? How do you know when you have found reality? How do you know why you are here and who put you here? He looked for these answers in three directions. First, he tried to find these answers by himself. If you try to do that you are making a big mistake because that is a very dead end. The second thing he tried to do was to find the answer to the meaning of life from other people – first by looking at them with his eyes, and second by listening to them with his ears and collecting proverbs.

Finally, at the end of his life, having believed vaguely in God all through his life, he began to wonder if God has the answer. He turned his eyes upwards and he realised that is where he should have begun. Isn't that tragic?

Let me just run through then the three phases of his search. Phase number one, which most of us go through especially when we are young, is this: I am going to find out the meaning and reality of life for myself. I am not going to listen to my parents; I am not going to listen to the oldies; I am going to try this, that and the other. I am going to try those things especially if I am told not to, until I have found out what real life is and what it is all about.

There are three parts to your personality and you can use every one of the three to try to find out for yourself what life is all about. This man acknowledges freely and honestly in chapters 1–2 that he would use every part of his personality to find out about real life if he could. He began by using his mind and he studied and got as much knowledge as he could. He packed his brain with every fact he could lay his hands on. He wanted to be a really clever young man and he found out that he did not discover life; the answers did not come. So he turned from his mind to his heart. He tried the search for happiness. He tried wine, women and song. He tried everything he could for pleasure and still it led nowhere. So having exhausted his mind and his heart he decided to try his will, and dedicated himself to achieving greater things than anybody else had achieved. With sheer determination he planted great estates and built great buildings, and he engaged in a public works programme to be remembered after he had gone for what he had achieved. Yet when he had done it all he thought: I still don't know why I'm here; life is a dead end. Now that is the end of phase one, and you find that at the end of that phase he discovered one thing and it is that God sets the timetable for your life. You cannot decide that next week you are going to be happy and the week after that not be happy. God sets the time and there is a time for dancing and a time for mourning. You do not know at this stage whether next week is going to be one or the other. Your times are in God's hands. The writer had tried by himself for so long to find the answer to life; now he realised that God had decided what his life would be like. God decided what time he did anything. God decided the time he was born, and God would decide the time he would die. Therefore, trying to find life by yourself without God is a hopeless quest.

So he moved from phase one into phase two. He began to wonder how other people were getting on with this search. Has anybody else found the answer to the question that is bothering me? He began first of all to use his eyes to look at how people behaved and what they discovered and how things happened in the world. He studied all kinds of life. He looked at wealthy people; he looked at poor people. He looked in the highest courts of the land; he looked in the lower courts too. He looked at all manner of people in their daily work and in their leisure. He looked at them as they killed themselves to make money. He looked at them as they were too lazy to repair their own roof. He scratched his head and wondered: what does that tell me about life?

He came to just two conclusions by observation. Number one: that life is very unjust, and that life does not seem to bear any relation to how good you are or how bad you are, as to whether you are healthy or wealthy. In fact he observed: wherever I look I see injustice; I see it in the courts, but I just see it in life generally. The good often suffer and the wicked get away with it. Then a man works hard and honestly all his life, he gets his money, then he dies and he leaves it all, and his son wastes it all; life is so full of injustice.

This began to get him right there, because if there is one thing that makes us more upset than another it is feeling something is unfair. It is the only conclusion you can come to if you just look at this life. Why is it that some people seem to go from one trouble to another, and others are relatively trouble free? It is not because these people are bad and those are good; it is unfair.

The other conclusion to which he came by looking at life was that life is an impermanent, fleeting thing. He became very much aware of death, the great leveller; the great enemy that puts us all in the dust. It does not matter whether we are kings or beggars.

So he came to these two conclusions by observation of other people: life is unfair and life is very short. So what do you do about life? He came to this conclusion: enjoy what you can while you can.

Somebody in my congregation had a meal in a restaurant and brought back the bill to show me. It lists the wine, the starters, main dishes and desserts, but at the top was printed: "A man has no better thing under the sun than to eat, to drink, and to be merry. Ecclesiastes." That was the conclusion the writer came to. Since life is so unjust and is passing quickly, and since for him death was the end and he could see nothing beyond but oblivion, he just didn't know what happened to a man when he died and he drew only one logical conclusion and that is to enjoy what you can while you can – and that makes sense.

I read this amazing sentence from Dag Hammarskjöld who was Secretary General of the United Nations: "In the last analysis it is our conception of death which decides our answers to all the questions that life puts to us." Isn't that a remarkable statement? For the writer of Ecclesiastes death was the end and oblivion. To this day in Israel death is the greatest tragedy. As Golda Meir said of the 1967 War: "The death of one Israeli is a disaster."

If you do not have a clear conception of what happens to

you when you die then what is there but to eat and drink and be merry? What are we doing in church? Let us make for the nearest disco, restaurant or bar, and let us enjoy ourselves.

But still this writer pressed on with his quest. Then he decided to explore other people's experience, using his ears. Perhaps the way to do it would be to collect proverbs. Proverbs are like potted, pithy pictures which seem to sum up and accumulate wisdom and all that people have learned. We listen to what other people have found to be true of life. They try to pass on to us in little sayings how to make the most of life, how to find the meaning in it, how to live every day of your life.

I saw that once in an autograph album. Somebody had written their signature, and above it they had written, "May you live every day of your life."

I thought, "What a funny thing to say." Then I thought further about it and realised that it was true. I once heard it said of a man, "He was dead at fifty though he was not buried till he was seventy," and I understood that one too.

So this writer started collecting proverbs. He made a kind of pocket treasury of words and wisdom, and this is the book of Ecclesiastes. He strung them together and he tested them in his own experience, and the things he thought were true he wrote down. They really read as a very strange mixture. In 10:1 for example – did you realise that little saying about the fly and the ointment came from Ecclesiastes? In the last verse of the same chapter 10 (a little bird will tell someone) – did you realise that came out of Ecclesiastes? These are little gems of wisdom that people pass on and say: now this is what I have found and this is how I have discovered life works.

So he collected the proverbs and said many good things. He discovered amongst other things that bad has a much greater influence than good. That is a sad fact of our world but it is true. Dirt spreads but cleanliness never does. Have you ever noticed that? You know if you wash one hand it doesn't get the other hand clean. But if you have got a dirty hand it can get the other one dirty. He noticed that disease is infectious but health is not, which means that in our world badness spreads much more quickly than goodness. Now that is worth learning. It is an observation, a proverb. The fly in the ointment – that is precisely what it is.

He also taught us that our mouths give us away, which always sobers preachers up, but also in conversation our mouths will tell other people whether we are wise or fools. I am reminded of another saying: It's better to keep your mouth shut and to be thought a fool than to open it and remove all possible doubt – which again is a proverb.

In the proverbs, he discovered from other people's experience that the world's values are often wrong way up. There is that little story about the town and the king: in the town there was a poor man who could have saved the town because he was a wise man, but nobody would listen to him because they said a poor man can't be wise or he'd have made money. They never listened, and the world undervalues poor people.

Then he would tell us that if you are going to invest, you had better spread your investments. I am not going to say more about that little bit, but he said: invest your money in foreign trade and you might make a bit of money these days. I will leave you to think that one through. He also taught us by collecting proverbs that a balanced attitude to work was needed; that if you either kill yourself for your work or if you are too lazy to work then you have not come to terms with what God meant to be a vital part of your life. He also taught us the need for foresight and a hundred and one other things by collecting proverbs. Then, having done this, having listened to other people, he came to two conclusions: one positive and one negative. The positive one was that proverbs were God-given, and that it is God's way of passing wisdom on from one generation to another, and we should praise God for them. Someone who cuts himself off from the advice of those who have lived before is a fool. These proverbs are God's way of shepherding us. The writer explains that they are such pointed sayings that they are just like the sharp stick that a shepherd uses to keep sheep in the track. In fact, they are so sharp in their points they are like sharp nails that fix something in place. In fact, God is using these proverbs to guide you in the right direction and to fix you in the right position. That is why these pointed sayings are so helpful. They sum up so much in one simple point. Now that was the positive thing that he found by listening to proverbs. The negative thing is that if you start studying proverbs you will never finish. There are so many such sayings.

This poor man, when he began listening to such sayings of other people, got overwhelmed with his library. I was a bit shattered to have a well-known publisher sitting in my congregation one day – one who was publishing a book I had written. Of the making books there is no end, and much study is of weariness to the flesh. The conclusion the writer of Ecclesiastes came to was that if you are really going to try to absorb all the wisdom of previous generations you will have an impossible task – your library won't be big enough. In fact, it says in John's Gospel that if everything Jesus did was written down, the whole world could not contain the books that would be written – that is just from one person.

The writer of Ecclesiastes felt that if you try to get the meaning of life by absorbing all the wisdom of the past, you will find there is too much to study and you will wear yourself out. I have met young people who have found this, and even older people who have said, "I'm going to study all the religions of the world until I come down on one. I'm going to read all the philosophers before I'll accept Christianity is true," and off they set on their quest. I have known people whose very grasp of reality has been shipwrecked because they have read too many books. They have studied too many philosophers; they have listened to too many religious teachers. Phase two (I'm going to get my answer from other people) comes to this disillusioned end.

Then he moved to phase three. The writer began to think he had always believed in God – did he have the answer all along? He finally wonders if he could pass on to the young generation, those at the beginning of life, just one thing that would put them on the right track – taking all that he had studied, all the proverbs, and all those bits and pieces of knowledge. Could he take all his personal experience and sum it up in just one sentence so that people could go away with one thing in their minds that would put their foot on the right path to make the most of life? He thought that he could. "Fear God and obey his commandments" – that is the answer. That is a very simple sentence. One of the things that strikes me about Ecclesiastes is that he never had any difficulty believing in God. He was a Jew and, like every Jew, he had God in his bones and in his blood. There was no explanation for the history of his people if there wasn't a God, and therefore he never had to argue for the existence of God, even with himself. He always knew there was a God and from the very beginning of Ecclesiastes God is there in the background. Had you noticed? But I am afraid that until the last page he is in the background. He is there but not in the forefront of attention. All through, as Ecclesiastes tells us of this man's desperate search for the meaning of life, God keeps being mentioned – always there – and yet he is not looking to God for the answer.

Now at the end of his life this simple question is posed: wouldn't God know why he put me here? Isn't that sensible?

Of course, if man is the result of a random mutation of chemicals, if man appeared, as some evolutionists believe, because some chemicals in a warm little pond had a lightning flash that did something extraordinary and brought them altogether utterly by chance, if man came about like that there is no meaning to life – it is absolutely absurd. Modern art, drama, and music would be right in saying that life is a sick joke, and there is no meaning; that you will never find the answer to the question. But if there is a God, and God made me, then he must surely know why I am here.

He came to the conclusion that the very best thing a man could do with his life was say, "God, will you tell me what to do, and I will do it and then I will know what life is all about." Nothing could be more sensible than that: that the person who put me here knows why I am here as an individual. One of the most remarkable things to me is that God doesn't look at people as I might look at you in a sea of faces. He sees one individual, and another, and he has put you here and he has a plan for you. If you just do what he says then you will find the meaning to your life and you will know why you are here. You won't have to search, you won't have to read all the philosophers, you won't have to collect all the proverbs – you will discover why you are here.

Ecclesiastes knew that people do not obey unless they have a strong enough motivation, and that there is that in our nature that doesn't like to be obedient to anyone else. There is something in us – the kind of cast iron muscle in the back of our neck – that does not bow down to anybody else, and that says, "I will do my own thing."

So what motive would be strong enough to make people do what God tells them? The writer can only think of one that is big enough, and that is fear. When people are afraid they act, and if only people were afraid enough of God they would do what he told them and they would discover the meaning of life. Now that was his theory, and it does not work because human nature neither fears God nor obeys him. Why do we not fear God? Because he does not settle his accounts every Friday; because he does not punish us fully in this world, and because it is not clear that God is our judge if you observe life in this world only. So Ecclesiastes collapses in its last verse. He tells us God is going to judge everything we do, even things done in secret, but who is afraid of this big God, and therefore who is obeying him? The answer is that human nature neither fears nor obeys by nature. These are two unmentionable four-letter words to fallen man. So we have got to leave Ecclesiastes. Wouldn't it be dreadful if we had to stop there and could say no more? Let me take you back to the very beginning. Why is it that Ecclesiastes never really, finally, got the answer? He nearly got it; he got the beginning: Fear God and obey him. That is the most marvellous starting point; it is the beginning of wisdom.

Put your foot there and you have put your foot on the path that leads in the right direction, but that was all he found and he could not get any further. He found the starting point at the very end of his life, but even had he found that starting point at the very beginning, he could not have travelled the path. Even had he come to the conclusion in his teenage years that the only way to live was to fear God and obey him, he still could not have managed it. Why? Because he lived within too narrow a frame. He said, "Beneath the sun and before I die" – and he looked at life from the inside and you can never see life properly from the inside.

I had a funny little picture in my mind when I was thinking "How can I get that across to a congregation?" I thought of myself as a little microbe wandering around in someone's body and trying to figure out what I had got myself into. Wandering up and down, having a trip down the alimentary canal and thinking, "Where does this lead to?" and going around in all the different cavities, passing the kidneys, the liver, and then getting up into the brain and thinking, "What is all this grey mass here?" I realised that as long as I was looking at this from the inside I would never know what it all was. I was locked within it, and only if I could somehow get outside and take a look at this from the outside would I realise: "Well, that is a human being."

It may seem a very silly illustration but one of the reasons why Ecclesiastes could not see the meaning of life, and why many cannot, is that they are beneath the sun and within the life that terminates in the grave. Within that framework you are inside life and you cannot see it. You can only see bits of it and you can only pick up little proverbs that apply to little aspects of life. You cannot see what it is all about. If we are ever going to get the answer we are going to have to get above the sun and beyond the grave. Then, of course, it will be too late to make the most of this life. Unless someone could come to us from above the sun and beyond the grave and say that he sees life from the outside; he sees what it is all about and he has got the answer.

The great news from the New Testament – and it is what makes a complete Bible – is that in Jesus Christ I have got someone who was above the sun, and comes to me from beyond the grave and says: "I am the life".

He reveals that the first thing you need if you are going to discover life is a new relationship to God. Ecclesiastes saw that God is your Creator, your Shepherd, your Judge. Jesus came from above, and from beyond the grave, and revealed that God is your Father – and life begins with that relationship.

I will never forget one of my most thrilling moments on my first trip to Israel. I heard a son running after his father and he was shouting, "Abba, Abba, Abba." Jesus taught that you can be so related to God that you can say "Abba, Father." To this day a Jew is afraid even to use God's proper name but a Christian is someone who says, "Abba, Dad, Father". There is a stronger motive now; the new relationship has given a new motive. The motive is: "Love God and keep his commandments."

Do you know there is only one motive that is stronger than fear? Here is a house on fire and here are the mother and father running away from that fire. They are afraid of that fire; their house is burning. Suddenly they turn around and they run back in. What motive has overcome their fear of being burned alive? The motive of love sent them back into that situation. The love for someone inside there has overcome their fear. Love is the fulfilling of the Law.

But there is something else going to be needed and it is that I am going to need a new nature – not just a new relationship, not just a new motive, I am going to need a new nature because the old me is quite incapable of ever keeping the commandments of God. Jesus came from above and he said: "I am the life". He can give you new life; a new nature. You can be born again from above; you can start life all over again. You can be a new you, and unless you do you never will see the kingdom – but you can.

Those three things came to me at a place just outside Jerusalem where Jesus died on a cross. It was when I went to that cross and found God in a new way that there came a new relationship with God not only as Creator, though he is that; not only Judge, though he is that; not even only as Shepherd, though he is that – but Father, Abba.

A new motive is born – not fear, but love. Father, you know everything; you know that I love you. Then he wants us to do as he tells us because of love.

There came a new nature – not the old one that did not like to be told what to do, but a new nature that could respond to

God's will. Ecclesiastes fades into the background. For us, we have found the answer and the questions are over. We no longer need to try to discover for ourselves what life is. We no longer need to discover from others their experience of life. Helpful though all these things may be in their place, we have found the answer in Jesus.

Read Ecclesiastes 11:7–12:8

Time is one of the most fascinating things and not the least of its fascinations is the speed with which it passes. All of us have the same amount of time in one day. We may not have the same amount of money but we have the same amount of time, yet for some people today has been a very long day and for others it has been a very short one. Sometimes time rushes by and sometimes it drags. In a hospital ward for the poor patients it drags on and on, from the first cup of tea at six o' clock in the morning or whenever, but for the nurses and doctors time doesn't drag, it flies by.

Here is a little poem *Time's Paces* by Henry Twells (1823–1900).

> When as a child I laughed and wept,
> Time crept.
> When as a youth I waxed more bold,
> Time strolled.
> When I became a full grown man,
> Time RAN.
> When older still I daily grew,
> Time FLEW.
> Soon I shall find, in passing on,
> Time gone.
> O Christ! wilt Thou have saved me then?
>
> *Amen.*

A later, amended version of the poem can be seen on a clock case in Chester Cathedral.

That is what time does to you. It doesn't just accelerate as you go through life but it goes slowly some days and very quickly on other days.

That is what this passage is talking about. It is contrasting two periods in life: youth and age. It is saying about youth that youth comes very slowly but it goes so quickly, and age comes so quickly but it goes so slowly. This is one of the stark contrasts of life, and this man is writing from the perspective of age. He is looking back down the years to his youth and he is so anxious to try to help young people to make the very most of the only life they will ever have on earth. So he writes from that background and you can almost hear a quavering old voice behind these words.

The first thing he does is to look at life generally and remind us what a tremendous gift it is – that whether you are young or old, every year is a blessing for which you ought to be grateful; every day is a gift. He describes the sheer bliss of opening your eyes to seeing the sun in the morning. Now that is not always something for which we remember to say thank you, but we are taught that every day you see the light you should say: "Thank you, Lord." It is another gift, another day that he has presented you with, another blank page of life on which you are going to write many things.

Be grateful for every year. Whether you are young or old, say: "Thank you Lord for this year, it is a lovely gift." Furthermore, he says what is very often true: that you will value life more if you remember that you will be dead much longer. In other words, it is a thought of death that makes life precious. Now of course we know that in his day he had no hope of anything beyond the grave. For him, death was oblivion; you went into nothing. The sheer hollowness for the future gave life a more precious quality. But even when you do have a hope for the future, as we have, nevertheless a brush with death can make life very precious.

I was talking to a minister who went out to Ethiopia for Tearfund and there contracted a frightful disease. He came home and was very near to death. Indeed, he went through one of those unusual experiences of his spirit being separated from his body, and of watching the doctors and nurses fighting for his body below him. Coming back from that experience he was very simply describing for me how precious life had become, how different his values were, how he saw his family through new eyes, and this realisation put life into a new perspective for him.

Now having looked at every year with deep gratitude for the sheer privilege of being alive, the writer points to a difference between being young and being old, and he makes a plea from an old man to every young person to consider carefully the great possibilities of their youth and to realise that it comes slowly but it goes quickly, and that age will come quickly but it will go slowly.

Isn't it strange that when we are young we are always wanting to grow up and wishing we were older. If you ask somebody who is fourteen and three quarters how old they are they will say, "I'm nearly fifteen." They want to rush on and grow up.

Ecclesiastes teaches: young people, you may wish you were growing up more quickly, but don't; value your youth. It is profound advice. He is saying it from his perspective: realising from his point of view that he has no hope beyond the grave, he looks back upon his life and concludes that the best days of his life were his youth. He pleads with young people to make the most of them. He doesn't present them as an old man with a long list of "don't"s. He presents them with some very positive "do"s. He points out that God has placed you in a fascinating world full of possibility, and these possibilities are to be explored and enjoyed, so do what you want to do. Surprising advice! Normally, young people look upon older people as those who say, "Don't do what you want to do."

Here is an old man saying: do what you want to do; explore that experience; enjoy all of life's possibilities. You are young; you are fit. Youth is not a time to be full of cares; it is a time to be carefree – so avoid pain if you can; avoid worry if you can.

It is not the time for income tax and rheumatism. It is the time to explore and enjoy. Here is a profound affirmation of life from this old man to young people, starting very positively.

There are some who would be horrified and say, "Now that is the worst possible advice you could give. You will lead young people into all kinds of trouble." Well, just take the whole of this old man's advice and the thing is put right. His message means: young people, you will only be young once and you will only be young for a short time and it will go quickly; so do what you want to do, explore life's possibilities, but remember God – don't just seek to get the most out of your youth but seek to put the Maker into it. Now that is what puts the advice right. Of course, this is the one piece of advice that is so necessary because the easiest time of life to forget God is in your youth.

That is why I have spoken to Sunday School leaders and Crusader group leaders. One Crusader group leader told me sadly that, as far as he could see, fourteen out of fifteen children who went through the class forgot God after they left it. Sunday School teachers will tell you that out of all the children in this country who have been through Sunday School, probably three out of four at a minimum forget God somewhere between the ages of twelve and fourteen. Why? The answer is: because life is offering so much else. There are so many places to go, so many things to do, so many people to meet. Suddenly a young person realises that they have got to get on and find experience and enjoy things because the world is so full of possibilities. It overwhelms you, and if you are not careful there are so many things to see, hear and do, that the unseen God doesn't get a look in, and he is forgotten. Indeed there is a reason why we may want to forget him, because we might feel that he is a little bit of a spoilsport, and that if we let him in on our youth then he is going to spoil it for us.

In Staffordshire, many years ago, we were talking to people on the streets and I spoke to a young man who was just about to go into a pub. I said, "You know, we've got some young people's meetings up the road, would you like to come and hear something about Christianity and about Christ?" We chatted away and he looked at me and said, "Religion? I'll tell you just what I think. While I'm young I want to see life. Maybe one day when I'm middle aged I'll come and listen, but while I'm young I want to see life." He somehow had gained the impression that God was going to spoil his fun. He was like children who say to parents, "You know, we'd like to have a party but we'd like you to go away for the evening."

But this wise writer, looking back on his youth, knew that if he had his youth again he would want to make the most of it and would want to get the Maker in it. So remember your Creator and remember too that he is not only the Creator but he is the Judge. If you remember those two things and keep those in mind then make the most of your young years – that is very positive and sound advice. Remember that God is your Creator. That means the life that you are living is not yours, it is his, it belongs to the Maker. Remember, too, that he issued you with a Maker's handbook on how to get the best out of it– the Bible.

Remember your Creator, but remember too that he is also your Judge; because this life he has given you is his and not yours and he will one day say: now give it back to me and tell me what you did with it. That is when the accounts are settled and the bills are paid. There is nothing in life more expensive than sin. It is so costly – it costs lives. It could cost any of us eternal life. It cost Jesus Christ his life – it is a terribly expensive thing and if you remember this then the account will not need to be paid.

Remember your Creator while you are fit, while you are exploring this fascinating world. When you are overwhelmed with all the things there are to do, and you want to try everything, just remember that it is God who made your life and God who will judge it, and then you will be all right. That is the old man's advice – very positive, very balanced, and very wise. I daresay that there are many who would want to say: I wish there was somebody who had really told me that when I was young.

Now he turns from looking at youth to looking at age. This is the second best known passage in Ecclesiastes. The best-known passage of course is in chapter 3 – a time for this, that, and the other. But I think this description of old age in chapter 12 is one of the most poignant and poetic passages in the whole Bible. It is beautifully written and indeed it is very sensitive and tender. Never have we had a more graphic description of the decay and ultimate disintegration of the human body.

When you are young you never dream somehow that you will be old. Have you had this experience? You look at old people and you think they are a different species, and that they have always been like that. My daughter was totally surprised one day when I told her what motorbike I had when I was young, and her eyes were like saucers. Me, on a motorbike? I was young once. A little boy said to his grandfather: "Grandpa, were you in the ark with Noah?" His grandfather said, "No I wasn't," and the little boy said,

"Then how come you weren't drowned?" So we have this kind of attitude: "Those are the old folk and they were born that way; they are old and I am young and I am going to stay this way and we are two different species."

But there comes a point, I don't know when it came for you first – you may remember it; I think it came for me first when I began my ministry. I remember one afternoon when I visited seven really elderly people. I came back from those seven visits and it suddenly hit me: you will one day sit where they sit. It was the first time I actually realised this. Ecclesiastes teaches us that it is a good thing to realise this. It paints very graphically a picture that you must paint for yourself so that you can remember your Creator in the days of your youth.

The final scene of the shattered well is a marvellous picture of the end of our human frames. The silver cord snaps, the jar is broken, the well from which you have drunk is now useless, nothing more can be drawn from it. All the drinks you have had are over; all the refreshment of life is finished. It is a picture of a deserted well from which has been drawn much water, but which now lies empty, idle. We learn that that comes quickly and it goes slowly. If you are young, remember this, and get a true perspective on life.

My daughters were at a school where it was arranged that the children had an elderly person to go and visit once a week. I think that was a great idea, helping both ways – helping to share both ends of life so there can be wisdom from the one and life and enthusiasm from the other. Now, in this rather sad description in chapter 12 there are two things that make it even sadder. Indeed your heart weeps not so much for the physical description here as for two facts from this man's thinking. One is that he cannot look forward with anticipation and the other is that he cannot look back with satisfaction. The one thing worse than growing old is growing old with this frame of mind which has nothing to look back on with satisfaction and nothing to look forward to with anticipation. What a terrible end of life! Once again, this man is absolutely honest. I don't think I have read such a courageous book of the Bible as this as I have studied it. Here is a man who faces facts squarely in the face and says that this is life as it is.

Look at those two things. First, he has nothing to look forward to with anticipation – because at that stage there had been no belief in life after death. Mustn't it be terrible getting older knowing there is nothing there? To think that a life that has once meant so much to other people, a life that has been so rich in experience, a life that has been so full – that that life should go into oblivion is to me unthinkable. On the gravestone of Green, a great historian, there are these words: "He died learning." There is something tragic about that epitaph – the knowledge that went into that man's brain, all the research, all the breadth of his vision – is all that to go to oblivion? Is it a tale told by an idiot signifying nothing? I just underline this sense of utter emptiness as he faces the future, because it is Jesus Christ who has changed that. If you and I were alive in the days when this man was alive we would have had to say: "There is nothing to look forward to."

There is another sad thing about this man's position as he looks back over his life and assesses what he has done. We saw in the earliest chapter that he tried the ways of enlightenment, knowledge, education, enjoyment; he tried every pleasure he could. He tried the way of enrichment, enlarging his wealth and building an estate. He tried so much, and at the end of it his epitaph for his own gravestone is one word: useless. It is all useless; all vanity. It has all been wasted; it has all come to nothing, because at the end of the day he had nothing to show for it but an empty well with a broken cord and a smashed water jar.

Now that is very sad and yet there are thousands of people who are reaching an old age in which they have nothing to look forward to with anticipation, and little to look back on with satisfaction. How utterly hollow and empty such a life can be. No wonder a man who is locked into that outlook pleads with young people: make the most of your youth, but do remember your Creator.

In my ministry experience I have come across some pretty rough quotations. I encountered a man in his late sixties who said: "I am determined to kill time as speedily as possible now that it has become my greatest enemy." Isn't that terrible? Ecclesiastes says, "Remember your Creator in your youth." The chances of your remembering him later are slim.

Did you come to know the Lord before you were twenty-five? It is important to remember the Lord when you are young because if you don't remember him then you are not likely to later. Many do, praise God. I think of one dear old lady who came to our old folks home in Chalfont St. Peter. She was ninety-four when she came. She was Britain's champion rifle shot and a sportswoman to her finger tips. Every morning, in her carpet slippers, she was running around the house outside. Then, after a week or two in our home, she said, "Have I got into a religious home?"

"Yes," we said.

She said, "Oh, I've never been religious all my life."

She came to know the Lord and was born again at that age. The next thing she said was, "Can I be baptised?"

So we said yes and we fixed her baptism. Just two weeks before she was due to be baptised, she just went to bed one night and woke up in glory. It is lovely when somebody of that age comes to the Lord and is given new life. But it is a rare thing. The time to remember your Maker is when you are young – otherwise you may forget.

Now let us turn to the Lord Jesus. There is not a mention of him in this passage, and again one feels the agony of a life that has to be lived as best it may without him. There is nothing to look forward to. "Useless, useless," says the Philosopher.

But as soon as you put the Lord Jesus Christ into the middle of life, the whole attitude changes. When you read the New Testament you find there is a totally different evaluation of life. Paul teaches: "For to me to live is Christ, and to die is gain. If I am to live in the flesh, that means fruitful labour for me. Yet which I shall choose I cannot tell. I am hard pressed between the two. My desire is to depart and be with Christ, for that is far better. But to remain in the flesh is more necessary on your account." The writer of Ecclesiastes is saying that he has nothing to look forward to. Paul can't wait to get there. Do you get the sense?

Here is one of the most lovely things that counteracts the pessimism of Ecclesiastes 12. Describing the decay of the outward man, Paul says: "Though our outer self is wasting away, our inner self is being renewed day by day. For this light momentary affliction is preparing for us an eternal weight of glory beyond all comparison, as we look not to the things that are seen but to the things that are unseen. For the things that are seen are transient, but the things that are unseen are eternal." You began that decay before you got halfway through your normal life span. Though my outward man is going downhill, my inward man is being renovated every day.

I went to see a man once and said to him, "How are you?"

He replied, "Well, the house in which I live isn't so good. The roof's leaking a bit now. The windows are getting a bit cracked, the door won't shut properly, but I'm fine." The outward man was decaying but the inward was being renewed.

I want to finish with what to me is one of the saddest stories in the whole of the Gospels. A young rich man had everything going for him and had reached the age when he realised that he was going to lose everything. He knew he would not keep his youth much longer. He reached the age when he could soberly realise that all his wealth would one day be left behind for someone else, if he had not already lost it. He realised that everything in his life that made life enjoyable, real and vital to him was going to be lost. So he went looking for eternal life, something that would last, something that would be worth keeping, a life that money couldn't buy. He went looking in just the right place; he went looking for a man called Jesus. He came up to Jesus: "Jesus, how do I get eternal life?" That was what he wanted to know – life that he could keep.

Jesus taught him that he needed to realise that he could not have everything in life, he had to choose. Nobody can have everything and in the case of this young man it was a choice between his money or his life. He could live now and pay later or pay now and live later, but he had come to a fork in the road and the decision he had to make was whether from then on Jesus was going to be in his life, and his life in him. The message was: go and get rid of your money, and come and follow me, and you can have life; a life that you can enjoy and keep for ever and ever.

That man was within an inch of eternal life and he said no. His face dropped and he chose to go back to a life that he would lose so quickly. It says that he went away looking very sad. He was sad because he couldn't have everything and he wanted everything; sad, because Jesus let him know that he could not have everything. There will be things that you will not have in your life if you have Jesus. There will be things that will have to go. Jesus was so honest with the people he met. He did not say that you can add him to everything else. No, he made it clear that some things have to go to make room for him. In this case it was the rich man's money. It isn't that in every case. But Jesus comes to a young person and the message is: if you want to do everything then you won't be able to fit me in; but if you fit me in, you can have eternal life.

Though the story does not tell me this, I also have a strong feeling that there were two very sad faces that day. As the young man turned away with a very long face, Jesus would have looked sad too. So a man who had everything presented to him turned it down to go back to his rich young life and forget his Saviour.

Make the most of your youth, enjoy it. But in your case, don't just remember your Creator and Judge, remember your Saviour, and remember the Lord who came that you might have life. That is what he wanted you to have. Jesus did not come to spoil our fun, he came that we might have life and have it more abundantly.

So if there is a young person reading this who is still wondering where real life is to be found, I beg you: remember your Saviour while you are still young. Before the years come when you forget him and you have nothing to look forward to with anticipation, and nothing to look back on with satisfaction, and the years come in which you say, "I have no pleasure in them now."

But I have talked to really old people, I think of one now, Anne Killingbeck. On my second last visit to her it was I think her 96th birthday. I made a rash promise and said, "Mrs Killingbeck, I'll come and see you on your hundredth birthday."

She replied, "I'll hold you to that" – and she did. A few years later she sent a message, "Come and see me on my birthday; I'm expecting you," and I had to travel six hundred miles to keep that promise. I have been very careful how

I have made promises since! But I went to visit one of the saints of God – really alive, vibrant, full of things to look forward to. She lived another year or two and then she went to glory, and she is enjoying herself more now than she ever did down here. "Remember your Creator" – and she had done so when she was a little girl. She had walked with him through the decades and she had known real life. She had not moved from the little cottage where she was born. The Lord had not called her to be a missionary. She stayed right there in that little Lancashire town, but how alive she was. Where is real life to be found? Ecclesiastes doesn't really have the answer. All he can say is: value your youth. Jesus invites us to come to him. He gives life that will last for ever and ever.